T0334239

Political Economic Perspectives of China's Belt and Road Initiative

The book begins with an overview on China's Belt and Road Initiative, highlighting its complex character as a domestic and international development strategy, and offering an up-to-date evaluation of it.

In response to this complexity, the book attempts to highlight the Belt and Road Initiative's double character and how it will address primary domestic development challenges that the Chinese government is facing by adding an international focus to a domestic development strategy. This in turn supports the understanding of China's political-economic policy and strategy formulation by reminding that supporting China's domestic development is still the primary task of its government. Even as the domestic aspect of the Belt and Road Initiative is highlighted, its regional and international relevance cannot be ignored either. The Belt and Road Initiative will support a continuation of the persisting debate about the impact that China's rise generates, and to what extent China can be characterised as a satisfied status quo power or a dissatisfied, revisionist power.

In this context, the book draws attention to the various impacts that the Belt and Road Initiative generates in different regional settings. However, the book also identifies some of the limitations that China's Belt and Road Initiative encounters, despite the seemingly convincing economic goals it offers, and explains why a few of the countries, like India, are resisting the lure.

Christian Ploberger is an independent academic researcher with research interests in international relations, regional integration, and climate change-related risks. The geographical focus of his research is on East Asia in general and on China specifically. He has visited East Asia regularly since 1993.

Routledge Focus on Public Governance in Asia

Series Editors:
Hong Liu, Nanyang Technological University, Singapore
Wenxuan Yu, Xiamen University, China

Focusing on new governance challenges, practices and experiences in and about a globalizing Asia, particularly East Asia and Southeast Asia, this focus series invites upcoming and established researchers all over the world to succinctly and comprehensively discuss important public administration and policy themes such as government administrative reform, public budgeting reform, government crisis management, public private partnership, science and technology policy, technology-enabled public service delivery, public health and aging, talent management, and anticorruption across Asian countries. The book series presents compact and concise content under 50,000 words long which have significant theoretical contributions to the governance theory with an Asian perspective and practical implications for administration and policy reform and innovation.

Translation and the Sustainable Development Goals
Cultural Contexts in China and Japan
Meng Ji and Chris G. Pope

The Two Sides of Korean Administrative Culture
Competitiveness or Collectivism?
Tobin Im

Political Economic Perspectives of China's Belt and Road Initiative
Reshaping Regional Integration
Christian Ploberger

For more information about this series, please visit www.routledge.com/
Routledge-Focus-on-Public-Governance-in-Asia/book-series/RFPGA

Political Economic Perspectives of China's Belt and Road Initiative

Reshaping Regional Integration

Christian Ploberger

Routledge
Taylor & Francis Group

LONDON AND NEW YORK

First published 2020
by Routledge
2 Park Square, Milton Park, Abingdon, Oxon OX14 4RN

and by Routledge
52 Vanderbilt Avenue, New York, NY 10017

Routledge is an imprint of the Taylor & Francis Group, an informa business

First issued in paperback 2021

© 2020 Christian Ploberger

British Library Cataloguing-in-Publication Data
A catalogue record for this book is available from the British Library

Library of Congress Cataloging-in-Publication Data
A catalog record for this book has been requested

ISBN: 978-0-367-18129-1 (hbk)
ISBN: 978-1-03-209068-9 (pbk)
ISBN: 978-0-429-05963-6 (ebk)

Typeset in Times New Roman
by Apex CoVantage, LLC

Dedicated to my uncle Erwin

Contents

Figures

Abbreviations

ADB	Asian Development Bank
ASEAN	Association of Southeast Asian Nations
BCIM-EC	Bangladesh-China-India-Myanmar Economic Corridor
BRI	Belt and Road Initiative
BRICS	Brazil, Russia, India, China, South Africa
CPEC	China Pakistan Economic Corridor
EEU	Eurasian Economic Union
EU	European Union
GDP	gross domestic product
GMS	Greater Mekong Subregion
HDI	UN Human Development Index
IMF	International Monetary Fund
NDRC	National Development and Research Commission
NPC	National People's Congress
PLAN	People's Liberation Army Navy
PM	prime minister
WTO	World Trade Organization

1 Introduction and overview

The challenge of grasping the Chinese government's 'One Belt – One Road' strategy begins with its name, as different descriptions exist (such as the 'Silk Road Economic Belt and 21st Century Maritime Silk Road') as do different abbreviations (such as 'OBOR' or 'BRI'). Since BRI now seems to become the rather accepted form for 'Belt and Road Initiative', it will be used in this book as the relevant abbreviation. Even if the description already indicates a kind of puzzle, describing its character offers an even greater challenge, as a wide range of related topics can be identified, such as: Does BRI signify a regional or geo-economic strategy, China's new grand strategy, or a national strategy to support development within China's remote and borderland areas? Or does BRI indicate China's challenge to the established international and political-economic architecture characterised by American and European interests? This latter aspect is associated with the enduring debate to what extent China is transforming from a rule follower to a rule maker in international politics, from a status quo power to a revisionist power. If the BRI is implemented fully, it will certainly increase China's regional and international influence and, as the document of China's National Development and Research Commission (NDRC), which does have government authorisation on the BRI highlights, the BRI will not only lead to a deeper integration of China into the world economic system but will also indicate that China is ready and willing to shoulder more global responsibilities and obligations, according to its capacities (Vision and Action 2015).

The enduring imagination of the memory of the ancient Silk Road also recalls various examples of past undertakings, which also offer a reference to the Silk Road metaphor to support more recent political-economic strategies, and to address development strategies, within the vast area of Central Asia. Some of them are the UNESCO project, 'Integral Study of the Silk Road: Roads Dialogue', which started in 1988; a UN Development Programme–backed 'Silk Road Revival Plan', which was launched in 2008; the

Japanese government's diplomatic efforts, described as 'Silk Road Diplomacy' in 2004; the American government's 'New Silk Road Initiative' in 2011, which, however, should be viewed mostly in the context of the ongoing operation in Afghanistan and how to sustain US operations there;[1] and the Kazakhstan government's announcement of a 'New Silk Road' strategy in 2012. In addition, there are also regional development programs which are sponsored by the Asian Development Bank (ADB), such as the Central Asia Regional Economic Cooperation Program, with a focus on transport, trade, and energy, or Russian strategies of trying to maintain close political-economic cooperation with the countries of Central Asia. Seen in this context, China's BRI neither was the first nor the only conceptual framework to engulf the Eurasian context, though it may be the most comprehensive one. Following such conception of space and historical context of the Silk Road metaphor, this book will address the regional context of the BRI by focusing on Central Asia, Southeast Asia, and South Asia; it will not include the part of the BRI which focuses on Africa.

On an abstract level, the BRI represents a transcontinental development strategy China initiated with a focus on supporting regional interconnectivity. However, the BRI also signifies the success of the Chinese reform process and that China has become a leading country at the global level. Indeed, the BRI is an indication of China's new-found economic strength and global political role. From its geographic focus, the BRI encompasses locations which have already been within the Chinese government's focus of interest for a considerable period of time, such as Southeast and South Asia, Central Asia, and Europe. Therefore, it seems to provide a political-economic framework to address related topics of closer cooperation of different geographic settings within a particular framework. Following such a line of consideration, one may understand the BRI as an umbrella of existing political-economic interests for the Chinese government. Trying to increase China's political-economic role in different regional settings consequently raises questions about the geopolitical and geo-economic impact this may generate on different regional settings. For sure, if the BRI is successful and comprehensively implemented, it would lead to a re-orientation of a good part of the global economy by generating a new political space based on the Eurasian continent. However, for the time being, we are quite far off from such a scenario, and the prospect for generating such an alternative political and economic space remains rather slim. Implementing the various infrastructure projects successfully would constitute a first but important step in such a direction.

At the same time, the BRI also inherits some limitations in its regional and global outlook, as it does not say much about the China-US or China-Japan relationship, nor does it address critical security challenges, such as that of the Korean peninsula. Even so, the BRI does represent one of China's vital foreign policy strategies by offering a framework for integrating various major aspects of its foreign affairs. Even so, one can characterise the BRI as one of China's central foreign policy strategies. Yet, this still would not be sufficient to describe entirely China's position, as this definition of the BRI would ignore China's domestic aspects, from a Chinese perspective, to address the economic imbalance we can identify among China's provinces, and would lead to a greatly misinterpretation of the BRI's nature. Once again, this would highlight the complexity of its character. A vital point not to be overseen is that China is still at a stage in which its development process should not be taken for granted; even exceptional success has already been achieved in both absolute and relative gains.

Even as China can rightfully celebrate 40 years of a successful reform process, in transforming a backward-looking country to one of the leading economic nations today, it still faces various development challenges, such as an increasing prospect of inequality in development between urban and rural areas and between provinces, and a continuing disadvantage of borderland areas. Even if geographic location represents an important factor, some of the underlying dynamics of this process of unequal development may even have been propelled by the reform process itself. In recognising this political-economic challenge, the Chinese government tried in the past to address this imbalance in development within China and continues to do so. Various economic and political strategies were adopted in the past but with rather mixed results, such as the 'Go West' strategy of the late 1990s and early 2000s, which should have supported a shift in investment and with it development from the eastern coastal areas towards the western parts of the country, including borderland areas, such as Xinjiang and Yunnan provinces. The strategic aim of such policy proposals was to address the geographical disadvantage those areas endured; yet those goals were only partially reached, and the disadvantage of the borderland areas continues today.

By taking into consideration China's continuous challenge in developing and in addressing an increasing imbalance in development, any major political-economic strategy the Chinese leadership formulates, even when it appears to have an overwhelmingly international character, would require addressing those domestic development challenges. It is worth remembering that supporting China's primary goal of development represents the utmost target for the Communist Party of China and China's government. Yet, at the same time, any major economic strategy should also support another long-stated national goal – that China, once again, become a strong and respected country at the global level. This strong link between domestic development and international recognition has been identified as the leading political-economic strategy since the now famous Third Plenary Session of the 11th Central Committee in December 1978. Certainly, if the BRI is implemented even partially, it will contribute to this overall strategic goal. Thus, when considering the BRI's strong emphasis on supporting domestic development within China, in addressing the uneven provincial development process, the BRI can be rightly interpreted as a national development strategy but one with a strong international focus added.

As such, the domestic relevance of the BRI for addressing China's own development outlook and challenges should not be ignored. This, in turn, put the BRI in a rather different perspective, when it is compared with the aforementioned geopolitical focus. However, the challenge of characterising China's BRI is that one can find arguments for both perspectives. After all, even if the BRI is implemented only partially, it will generate a dynamic of re-arranging economic geography within the Eurasian landmass and on various regional integration processes as added incentives for regional economic cooperation are generated. Even if this may be seen as a rather remote perspective in the context of a contemporary ocean-focused global economy, it would not be unprecedented historically, since over an extended historical period in history, land-based trade existed within the Eurasian context.

1.1   Taking stock of the Belt and Road Initiative

The origin of the BRI is widely attributed to comments President Xi Jinping made in September 2013 during a state visit to Kazakhstan. Indeed, on that occasion he proposed closer economic cooperation with Central Asian countries by forming an economic belt along the historical Silk Road. He stated that it was a foreign policy priority for China to develop a close and cooperative relationship with the countries of Central Asia (Xi Jinping 2013a). At that stage, the emphasis and focus of Xi Jinping's statement were oriented towards closer and deeper relations between China and Central Asian countries. By applying the historical metaphor of the Silk Road and by emphasising connectivity, Xi Jinping put renewed emphasis into a looser regional cooperation between Central Asian countries and China, thus supporting a regional integration dynamic. This approach on adding a renewed emphasis on a specific regional integration process also applies to Xi Jinping's address to the Indonesian Parliament in October 2013, when he referred to the Maritime Silk Road. This time the regional context on which he was focusing was Southeast Asia or, more specifically, the relationship with the Association of Southeast Asian Nations (ASEAN). In his address to the Indonesian Parliament, the overwhelming emphasis was on strengthening China-Indonesian and China-ASEAN relations even further, by supporting

ASEAN internal development and its role as a regional organisation, and by offering a closer economic and political cooperation (Xi Jinping 2013b). Even before Xi Jinping's speech at the Indonesian Parliament, Prime Minister Li Keqiang had already made a reference to the Maritime Silk Road at the 10th China-ASEAN Expo, in September that same year. He, too, mentioned the BRI in the context of addressing regional cooperation, like the ten-year-old China-ASEAN strategic partnership, by emphasising that China and the ASEAN were facing a similar development challenge and, thus, were natural partners, consequently stressing further closer cooperation (Li Keqiang 2013).

Since then, it has become known as the BRI extended in both scope and scale, and now includes 70 countries, covering 62 percent of the global population and 30 percent of global gross domestic product (GDP) (World Bank Brief 2018). Hence, the BRI represents an ambitious undertaking of regional cooperation on a transcontinental scale, the largest initiative to improve global connectivity to date. On an abstract level, among its participants the BRI supports infrastructure developments, a closer policy coordination with a focus on development, support for trade, and closer people-to-people contact within specific regional but also transcontinental levels. Another important step in outlining the character of the BRI occurred in 2015, when China's NDRC published an official document which had the State Council's authorisation and outlined the BRI in more detail. The document included a comprehensive evaluation of the focus and strategies of the BRI. The main aspects are centred on five features: policy coordination, facilitating connectivity, unimpeded trade, financial integration, and people-to-people connection. Further, the document also emphasises generating mutual respect and trust, mutual benefits, and win-win cooperation. Indeed, cooperation should be encouraged through consultation so the development interests of all participating countries are realised (Vision and Action 2015).

Thus, by facilitating closer interconnectivity between the participating countries, economic development will be facilitated, as will political cooperation and regional economic integration. On various visits to Central Asia and Southeast Asia, the author of the present book experienced that interconnectivity still represents a challenge for development. Such an observation holds true even when observing the fundamental changes that are already taking place. From such a perspective, one has to support the BRI project. An excellent example of the impact on infrastructure development is the fast progress made in connecting China's Yunnan province with Southeast Asia and with the Greater Mekong Subregion (GMS) in particular. Even so, the infrastructure challenge throughout Asia will continue for a considerable time, based on the ADB's assessment, which points towards an existing infrastructure investment gap of 2.4 percent of the projected regional

GDP for the 2016–2020 period (Meeting Asia's Infrastructure Needs 2017). A recent World Bank report also states that one main economic challenge for developing countries is missing logistic infrastructure, as this increases the costs for companies and thus negatively impacts their willingness to invest in those developing countries (Wiederer 2018).

Hence, existing gaps in intraregional connectivity need to be addressed first and, with it, the development of core infrastructure gains priority. In turn, this gives considerable support for any undertaking to promote infrastructure development. In this regard, it is possible to identify various aspects which make the BRI an attractive option for many countries. After all, a reliable road and rail network offers considerable economic development for a country as well as for its region. Importantly, once a reliable infrastructure has been built, it will offer a connection not only to the Chinese but also to the global market, thus overcoming an economic challenge which Central Asian countries are still facing. China's engagement with Central Asia through its BRI highlights that the BRI supports country-specific development goals, as is the case with Kazakhstan. Kazakhstan's government has a strong focus on infrastructure development, as the previous 'Kazakhstan 2030' and the current 'Kazakhstan 2050' development strategies indicate. Besides, the 2015 Joint Declaration on the China-Kazakh strategic partnership emphasised that China's BRI and Kazakh's development focus complement each other and contribute to a further deepening of their relationship (Joint Declaration 2015). This position was repeated in President Nazarbayev's 2018 state of the nation address, by pointing out that the comprehensive strategic partnership with China was gradually developing with the BRI, offering additional impulse for it. An added aspect is that Central Asian states have some desire to became more independent in their overreliance on Soviet area infrastructure, which links them strongly to Russia but offers only limited access to global markets.

Although infrastructure investment takes on a prominent role, not only as a perception, because much international attention is directed towards those infrastructure investments China has undertaken, we should not ignore that infrastructure development only represents a first step towards a closer economic cooperation among the participating countries. Yet one can rightly point out that, despite all the challenges infrastructure development may encounter, finalising trade agreements and treaties for regional economic cooperation and integration represent an even stiffer challenge. Undoubtedly, supporting a closer economic integration of various regional settings represents an essential part of the BRI and of the generation of the envisaged economic benefits. Hence, we may describe the construction of infrastructure connectivity and economic corridors as the arteries of the BRI, while the formation of closer economic cooperation will offer more substance by providing the glue for the whole integration development which underlies the BRI. This fundamental relevance of infrastructure connectivity was also highlighted during the Second Belt and Road Forum in Beijing in April 2019. In his opening address to this event, Xi Jinping (2019) emphasised that connectivity is crucial for advancing Belt and Road cooperation, and infrastructure forms the bedrock of connectivity, common development, and prosperity. The Joint Communique (2019) of the Second Belt and Road Forum also stresses the fundamental importance of transport infrastructure for connectivity and cooperation.

When taking into account the proposed economic corridors, we can start to appreciate the geographical extent the BRI is covering. To date, we can identify six economic corridors: the China-Pakistan Economic Corridor; the China-Mongolia-Russia Economic Corridor; the New Eurasian Land Based Economic Corridor; the China-Central Asia-West Asia Economic Corridor; the China-Indochina Peninsula Economic Corridor; and the Bangladesh-China-India-Myanmar Economic Corridor (BCIM-EC). Even if the corridors offer a good indication of the geographic and regional focus of the BRI, they rather symbolise a focused perspective, as focusing on economic corridors masks, to some extent, more regional and subregional attention within the BRI and, indeed, of the Chinese foreign policy, predating the BRI initiative but now being part of it. In this regard, the China-Indochina Peninsula Economic Corridor offers a good example. Although from an abstract perspective it makes sense to interpret it as a single economic corridor, such a perception is less appropriate from a more regional and subregional perspective, since it would ignore the long-established China-ASEAN strategic partnership as well as China's specific interests on the GMS integration process. The identification of the China-Mongolia-Russia Economic Corridor and of the New Eurasian Land Based Economic Corridor provides other examples. Here again, even if an abstract description of both corridors is helpful and offers some indication of potential economic integration, a more regional perspective, with a focus on Central Asia, would propose a more distinctive interpretation of the role the BRI can take in supporting China's position within this area. After all, China's engagement with Central Asia is quite complex, including bilateral and regional cooperation, as well as the China-Russia relationship. Once again, those relations and the related dynamics are predating the BRI initiative. Moreover, one could argue that the BRI, to some extent, may be even developed as a response to address China's complex political-economic interest in Central Asia and the competing interest with Russia over this geopolitical space.

Considering the BRI from a transcontinental perspective provides a comprehensive view about its dimensions. However, it is a rather abstract perspective, and as the above examples indicate, those economic corridors are based on long-established and regional-specific policy strategies of the Chinese leadership. Such reasoning supports a characterisation of the BRI as a strategic umbrella for various and long-established policies of the Chinese leadership instead of interpreting the BRI as China's new grand strategy. The author debated this subject in an earlier paper, which represented a first reasoning of the development of this book project (Ploberger 2017). With regard to identifying the impact the BRI has already generated, China's Ministry of Commerce has pointed out that, between January and October 2018, Chinese companies invested \$11.9 billion in 55 countries which are linked to the BRI, with an upward trend, as this amount is 6.4 percent higher than the amount which had been invested the previous year (MOFCOM 2018). Another way of assessing the impact that has been generated so far for Eurasian interconnectivity is the increasing frequency of freight trains travelling between China and Europe and a diversity of destinations they are reaching in both Europe and China. For example, the number of freight trains connecting different Chinese cities, such as Chengdu (Sichuan) or Zhengzhou (Henan), with cities in Europe is increasing steadily. In the case of Chengdu, there were 1,442 trains in 2018, which represents an increase of 117 percent over the previous year (Belt and Road Portal 2019a). In the case of Zhengzhou, which is located in central China, the number reached 752 trains, which indicates an increase of 50 percent over the previous year, with transported goods weighting 350,000 tons and a combined value of \$3.2 billion (Belt and Road Portal 2019b). Additional methods allow assessing the increasing relevance the BRI has achieved so far. A recent World Bank report points out that the significance of the countries which are linked to the BRI as a group has increased in global trade, as their share in global export has risen to 37 percent in 2015 while their share in global imports has increased to 21 percent. Further, their intragroup share of exports has grown to 44.3 percent in 2015 (Boffa 2018). Considering this and future potential economic impacts, the prospect that the BRI will contribute to more global trade cannot be ignored.

As Baniya et al. (2019) re-emphasised in another recent World Bank research report regarding infrastructure connectivity, the impact the BRI has generated on upper-bound trade (where trade can easily switch transportation modes) can generate an estimated increase of 4.1 percent, while with lower-bound trade (where trade cannot switch easily between different transportation modes) the estimate is a rise of 2.5 percent. In addition, when complementing the BRI's infrastructure improvements with trade reforms and better border management, trade could be boosted between 7.9 percent and 12.9 percent (Baniya et al. 2019, pp. 3–4). A recent RAND report argues likewise, pointing out that a lack of existing infrastructure among the BRI countries undermines their trade development potential; thus, the promised investments that are associated with the BRI are targeting countries which are most in need of such investments (Hui et al. 2018, p. 44).

Similarly, a recent International Monetary Fund (IMF) report highlights the positive economic effects of the BRI by stating that its successful implementation could facilitate greater regional integration and support economic growth, as long as the scale of investment does not compromise on debt sustainability of the involved countries (Regional Economic Outlook 2018, p. 13). IMF Managing Director Christine Lagarde offered a positive view on the potential of the BRI on several occasions, such as in 2017 and 2018, by identifying three benefits from its implementation: it would help to reduce the $1.5 trillion infrastructure gap of the developing countries; it would support inclusiveness within those countries by offering better connectivity to markets and public service; and it would support a stronger regional and international economic integration, thus generating more trade and economic growth (Lagarde 2017). In another speech in 2018, Lagarde again emphasised the positive capacity the BRI holds for the development of participating countries, citing the Thailand-China high-speed railway project and a manufacturing development zone in Kazakhstan as good examples for the transformative impact a modern infrastructure can generate. However, on this occasion, she also addressed some potential challenges to the BRI, such as the issue of debt burden and project implementation challenges. Hence, BRI-related projects should focus on the gaps in much-needed infrastructure and take the financial capacities of the involved countries into account (Lagarde 2018).

Yet the World Bank and the IMF are not alone in pointing towards potential positive economic impacts the BRI generates. Indeed, UN Secretary-General António Guterres indicated that China's BRI also shares the Sustainable Development Goal vision for global development, by creating economic opportunity, and by supporting national and regional cooperation (Guterres 2017). Besides, the director of the Development Policy and Analysis Division of the UN Department of Economic and Social Affairs, Ping-fan Hong, states that in implementing the UN 2030 Agenda – to eradicate poverty and hunger – forming global partnerships is a critical requirement for achieving this goal, and China's BRI offers an open and comprehensive strategy for international development cooperation (Hong 2017).

Despite those positive assessments about the potential of the BRI from non-Chinese sources, we can also identify critical voices related to the implications of the BRI for participating countries. These critical positions, in turn, raise the topic of risk evaluation and assessment in general but also from a Chinese perspective. Indeed, under-performance or mis-performance of BRI-related projects can undermine the perception of the BRI and, consequently, challenge the required cooperation among the involved countries for a successful implementation of the initiative.

1.2   Critical voices and assessing risks

Even though currently (at time of writing) about 70 countries are listed as participants in the BRI, various critical voices are increasingly heard. Certainly, there are the voices of China's regional and global competitors, such as India, Japan, and the United States, who are emphatically pointing out that geopolitical motivations alone drive China's BRI. Some of the strongest comments are related to the maritime part of the BRI, such as the Gwadar port project in Pakistan or the Hambantota port project in Sri Lanka, with accusations that China, in the disguise of economic cooperation, actually expands its military and geopolitical influence. The argument is that in the near future the People's Liberation Army Navy (PLAN) will use these port facilities as a basis for long-distance missions and, as such, will extend its operational capacity considerably. However, the Chinese leadership consistently denies such accusations. In this regard, a statement from China's foreign minister, Wang Yi, points out that the BRI should not be interpreted as expansionism, because it is an open initiative and not a kind of Chinese 'Monroe Doctrine'. The BRI constitutes a response to the development needs of Asian and European countries (Yi 2016).

For the time being, there are no indications that a continuous military use of those port facilities is planned by the PLAN or that such a use is part of any BRI investment agreement. However, it should not be ignored that the PLAN is extending its reach, and the process of building a so-called blue-water navy is well underway. It is also noteworthy that the 2015 version of China's Military Strategy paper states that seas and oceans contribute to China's sustainable development and lasting stability. Consequently, securing its maritime rights and interests are a critical task for its navy. Accordingly, the PLAN aims to shift its focus from 'offshore defence' to a combination of 'offshore defence' and 'open sea protection' that will enhance its maritime capabilities for strategic deterrence and maritime counterattack (Chinese Military Strategy White Paper 2015). This shift in strategy is a first step for China, which, over most of its history, has been a continentally focused land power. Such a shift in focus has certainly not gone unnoticed by other regional and global powers and competitors. However, it should also be mentioned that China's 2015 Military Strategy also recognised that the world has become increasingly interconnected and that multipolarity and economic globalisation bind countries together. As a result, this generates a shared destiny and offers a favourable international environment for China's own development (Chinese Military Strategy White Paper 2015). Yet, in his

Work Report to the 19th National Party Congress, Xi Jinping (2018) pointed out that one strategic goal for the period between 2035 and 2050 is that China will become a global leader in terms of composite national strength and international influence. In this context, it would be rather challenging to argue that the BRI, as one of China's most important strategies, would not be aligned to that goal. This statement gives additional impetus for interpreting the BRI in a geopolitical context.

While this offers a first indication of the criticisms the BRI encounters from a geopolitical perspective from regional and global actors, there are also some critical voices associated with the financial aspects of BRI-related infrastructure projects. So far, a small number of countries which are already taking part in the BRI are having second thoughts about BRI-related infrastructure investment to which they agreed previously. This is taking place even though improved infrastructure connectivity offers the potential for further economic development and, thus, can contribute to regional stability within different regional settings. Yet, most of the criticism is related to the cost associated with the debt that infrastructure investment loans, which China has offered, have generated. Within this category of criticism, we can identify countries such as Malaysia or Sri Lanka, and even Pakistan – a long-time ally of China and a major recipient of support within the BRI framework. A more detailed evaluation of these critical voices will be provided in the following chapters. Nevertheless, it is important to recognise that all of them are occurring in the aftermath of changes in the government of those countries. The new governments are reaching a different conclusion about the costs and benefits of some infrastructure projects. In addition, challenges exist in quantifying economically the short- and long-term impacts of infrastructure investment at the national level, even if the previously mentioned World Bank, IMF, and ADB evaluations strongly suggest that infrastructure connectivity represents a critical aspect for economic development. In this regard, McCartney (2018) offers an insightful observation by pointing out that, although there is a general recognition that BRI-related investments (e.g. the CPEC in Pakistan) have the potential to generate a transformational impact, it would require development state capacity, such as a professional and independent bureaucracy, to utilise the utmost from such investments. Yet, McCartney assesses that the Pakistani state lacks this capacity.

McCartney only refers to the Pakistani case. Nonetheless, the lack of state capacity of the countries participating in China's BRI represents an important aspect, especially considering that the Chinese government has repeatedly underlined that BRI-related investments should generate a long-lasting positive development impact. However, it would be wrong suggesting that it is the overall responsibility of the Chinese government to ensure that individual governments' administrative responsibilities and capacities are met by the recipient countries. This would even amount to infringement in domestic affairs of the recipient country and certainly would be not only unwelcomed but also a stated position of non-intervention of the Chinese government. The preceding examples indicate that the BRI is faced by a number of political and economic risks which may not have been assessed as thoroughly as required. Further, it seems that risk assessment at country and business level may become a higher priority for the Chinese government, within the BRI framework. In this context, it is interesting to note that Wang (2018), who is rather emphatic in his positive evaluation on the BRI, offers some second thoughts when it comes to the issue of risk evaluation. Indeed, this author argues that it should deserve more attention in general, and especially with regard to sovereign debt risk of the involved countries; he adds that China is rather lacking an in-depth understanding of the countries which are involved in the BRI.

Importantly, most participating countries in the BRI are developing countries and in the process of transformation. This, in turn, has increased political and economic risks associated with large-scale infrastructure investment. Clarke (2016) debates another aspect of ambiguity related to the BRI investments: China's rising role as an economic actor has been rather welcomed by Central Asia's political and economic elites, while among the public the perception of China's activities is more ambivalent. As a result, this could also generate some political-economic backlash for China if it is exploited by political-economic actors within those countries. In this view, the complexity and risk which are associated with the BRI become increasingly obvious. Yet from a Chinese perspective, another aspect needs to be considered. Indeed, as the BRI leads to further expansion of China's global role and within different regional settings, China has become more exposed to a variety of so-called traditional security risks. The violent attacks on Chinese workers in Pakistan's Balochistan province and on its consulate in Karachi provide some good evidence for it. Those attacks were directed against a major BRI related project, the CPEC, worth US$62 billion. It is necessary to point out, though, that Balochistan has already witnessed a long-running violent insurgency against the central Pakistan state, with the local Baloch people complaining that the province is exploited by the central government, while locals are denied their fair share of the province's rich resources. As such, China's BRI investment projects are getting mixed up with a long-existing local-central government conflict within Pakistan, as both attacks have been carried out by the Balochistan Liberation Army. A possible implication could be that China's security agencies, its policy, and its military may become more active abroad, as the 2011 incident on the Mekong River indicates. After an attack on a Chinese cargo ship on the Mekong River in October 2011, in which 13 Chinese sailors were killed, China became involved in policing the river in cooperation with law officers from Laos, Myanmar, and Thailand. It is an international cooperation in response that has dealt with various aspects of crimes (e.g. robbery, the drug trade, and human trafficking) to improve security along a stretch of the Mekong waterway. Nevertheless, it provides an indication of China's expanded law enforcement activities which go beyond China's borders and, thus, offers an indication of its extended political and security reach.

1.3 Chapter descriptions

Chapter 2 will address the BRI in the context of China's rise and to what extent the BRI can be identified as China's new grand strategy. An enduring and associated debate concerns to what extent China still represents a satisfied status quo power, accepting the existing international system which was not its making, or if China has become a revisionist country, aiming at undermining, and eventually changing, the existing international system. Even if this discussion about China's intention is not a recent one but has represented an ongoing discourse for the last 30 years or so, the BRI adds an additional dynamic for at least three reasons. First, the BRI offers another clear indication of China's increasing economic strength and leverage. Second, the BRI's comprehensive focus also indicates a very strategic approach for increasing China's political-economic weight in various regional settings and, consequently, on a global level. Thus, the BRI contributes to the growing capabilities of a rising country. Third, if the BRI is successfully implemented, it will offer a considerable challenge for the existing international order by generating a different geo-economic and geopolitical space based within the Eurasian context. Besides, as the BRI will be land based, it will also present a challenge to the existing focus on maritime trade. In this comprehensive outlook, the BRI also attracts attention as China's new grand strategy. However, as the author will outline in detail, the BRI has not all the characteristics for a grand strategy. For the time being, China does not represent a revisionist power, since it has quite extensively profited from the existing international system and still requires a stable international environment for addressing its own development challenges.

Chapter 3 will focus on the domestic aspect of the BRI, emphasising that, despite a lengthy and quite successful reform process, China continues to face development challenges such as an imbalance of development among its provinces. This imbalance transcends a mere economic aspect as it has a rather comprehensive character, related to remoteness, as several Chinese provinces are located away from the eastern coastline. Remoteness matters, as China's western and south-western border areas were not so long ago characterised as 'dead ends'. The cases of Xinjiang and Yunnan offer good examples of the challenges such provinces are facing and the potential support the BRI may offer for their development. From such a perspective, the BRI can be identified as a domestic development strategy but with an international focus. As a result, transnational cooperation should be supported via deeper integration of Xinjiang with Central Asia and Yunnan with Southeast Asia.

Chapter 4 will focus on another critical aspect, that is that the BRI can become a success with the willingness to cooperate by other countries. Even if China's BRI offers vital support for infrastructure development to its potential partners, not all are ready to participate in it. In this regard, India is a good example. Although it would require some of the infrastructure investment the BRI is offering, India is quite reluctant to participate in it. Nevertheless, this reluctance is linked to India's own perception as a regional power, so it does not perceive China's increasing presence in South Asia, which is interpreted as India's own 'backyard', as positive. However, we can also identify some countries that have been taking part in China's BRI but are now reconsidering their engagement because of economic evaluations. It is important to notice that such a reconsidering of the value of BRI-related investments occurred, in most cases, in the aftermath of government change in those countries. This reminds the reader of the political risks with which the BRI is confronted. Finally, with regard to BRI-related infrastructure investments in Europe, a diverse set of responses can be identified. On the one hand, Central and Eastern European countries are quite forthcoming in accepting them, while at the European Union (EU) level and among the leading European countries, China's BRI-related infrastructure investments are seen more critically. However, for the time being, it seems that the EU and China have established an accord.

Chapter 5 will assess the BRI from a more theoretical perspective with regard to regional integration processes. A rather general assumption is that contemporary regional integration processes are called 'bottom-up', non-state-guided projects, where below national level actors, provincial or local level actors are taking the most active part in supporting regional integration dynamics. This focus on the subnational level as a source for regional integration processes differs from earlier integration dynamics, in which the states took on the leading role and such integration projects were described as 'top-down' processes. Yet, it seems China's BRI represents another 'top-down', state-led integration process, thus offering a challenge to the aforementioned assumption that 'bottom-up' regional integration processes are the dominant form of contemporary integration dynamics.

1.4 Summing up: the Belt and Road Initiative between prospect and challenges

On an abstract level, the BRI represents a transcontinental development strategy China initiated with a focus on interconnectivity and on closer economic cooperation. This already indicates the extended geographical context it covers and the high number of topics which need to be addressed in implementing it. Thus, in turn, this highlights the complexity of the initiative and the challenges it will encounter during its implementation process. Beside this complexity, the various projects within this initiative also need the approval of the participating countries. Thus, investments, so far overwhelming infrastructure investments, need to be interpreted as relevant by China and the specific country in question. Even if the Chinese leadership repeatedly states that aligning China's and the host countries' interests is a precondition for identifying an investment proposal within the BRI, it would not come as a surprise that occasionally different opinions would exist. However, despite this challenge of complexity, we can identify an ongoing process of implementing various infrastructure projects related to the BRI. Further, the fact that the implementation of the projects takes place in quite different geographic locations gives the impression that the BRI is progressing on an intercontinental scale. Such an impression may have much to do with the character of the BRI, as an umbrella for previous existing political-economic strategies of the Chinese leadership. As such, many cooperation involving the BRI are not genuinely new, though the BRI may lead to a new emphasis on various investment projects and on supporting a deeper cooperation within different regional settings. Undoubtedly, if the BRI is implemented successfully, it will transform the Eurasian area by integrating a geopolitical and geo-economic space which so far has been characterised by disintegration. However, for the time being, such a prospect is rather remote.

Indeed, there are also signs that the BRI is encountering increasing challenges, although the implementation of projects is continuing and new projects are being added. Questions arise about the economic viability of some investments, especially in the context of government changes in some countries. Even if such reconsideration is related to domestic politics, it raises concern about the quality of political-economic risk assessment on the part of the Chinese government when selecting specific projects. This aspect of risk assessment may become even more important when the observer considers that generating infrastructure connectivity forms an albeit important first step, as economic cooperation and integration are equal critical goals within the BRI. In addition, some countries (e.g. India), which have been invited to participate and which could economically profit from infrastructure development are not interested in doing so. Taken together, these aspects are generating a considerable challenge for the implementation of the BRI.

From a Chinese government perspective, another aspect with regard to the BRI will be significant. Indeed, it is crucial to explore to what extent the BRI will address not only domestic development but also the development imbalance which is observable among China's provinces. These areas include borderland regions and remote provinces located away from the eastern coastal region and at the lower end of the development scale. After all, there is continuous reference from the Chinese leadership and official publications related to the BRI that an important task of the BRI is to address this development imbalance. There are early indications, though, that the BRI will offer support for this domestic development goal, but it is still an open question if this support will be sufficient to overcome the development gap we can identify among China's provinces.

Note

1 See Mankoff (2013).

2 The Belt and Road Initiative in the context of China's rise

China's BRI offers strong indication of China's new-found economic strength, as China can rightfully celebrate 40 years of successful reform process, which transformed a rather backward country into one of the strongest economies in the world. As the data in Figure 2.1 on China's GDP growth indicate, the reform process has been quite a success story, with some positive effects identifiable from the mid-1990s onward. From the mid-2000s onwards, the effect was quite astonishing, with China overtaking the UK and Japan in economic size, and continuing to increase. The BRI offers not only another indication of China's new-found economic strength but also takes into consideration the potential political-economic implications of a successful implementation of the BRI. It would support China's position in various regional settings and consequently also contribute to China's position on a global level. In this view, one could consider that the BRI

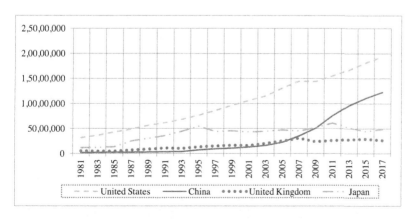

Figure 2.1 GDP in current US$ (millions)
Source: Derived from World Band data sets.

represents China's new grand strategy. This is confirmed when we consider that a grand strategy embodies an articulated statement of national strategic objectives, a broad statement of strategic action which guides policies in pursuing and implementing those priorities within a rational framework and over an extended period of time.

A related topic, both to China's incredible economic rise and in identifying the BRI as China's potential new grand strategy, is linked to the enduring discourse on whether China represents a status quo or a revisionist country – a rule-following or a rule-creating power. Besides, increasing economic strength also generates political implications by contributing to the political power of a state. As is the case with China, a huge country with an enormous population and added considerable economic strength, the topic presents itself as to what extent China will be still satisfied with its regional and global positions based on its lesser successful pre-reform period development path. Such profound questions arise in the context of China's rise, since the millennia-old process of great power change seldom was a peaceful affair. Although this discussion about China's new-found economic and political strength, its regional and global implications, and its ambition has continued almost uninterrupted since the reform process began, the BRI offers another important contribution to this debate, not least because of its scale and the potential of economic and political changes which are associated with it. After all, the BRI has the potential of generating a major re-direction of global trade, from a current focus on maritime trade to land-based trade, even though such economic re-alignment seems less likely for now. However, we should remember that there was a time in human history where land-based trade over an extended Eurasian space was all but the prevailing character of long-distance trade.

This chapter will explore to what extent the BRI would fulfil the characteristics to be identified as China's new grand strategy, and (an ongoing debate) to what extent China represents either a satisfied or non-satisfied power in the ascent.

2.1   Grand strategy, national interests, and the Belt and Road Initiative

Assuming that governments and national leaders rule a country not on a day-by-day basis, we can anticipate that national leaders are pursuing some kind of strategy when in power, with Luttwak pointing out that 'all states have a grand strategy, whether they know it or not' (Luttwak 2009, p. 409). After all, defining and implementing a grand strategy is not a novel undertaking in the history of international relations, as advancing concrete national interests, which are domestic and international in the context of a geostrategic environment, are not only the purposes of formulating a grand strategy but are at the essence of politics.

When considering identifying the BRI as China's new grand strategy, we should begin with a definition of grand strategy, as most economic and political concepts undergo various re-interpretations and re-contextualisation over time.

Hart (1967, p. 322) points out that the term 'grand strategy' was traditionally associated with war and how best to mobilise and coordinate forces and resources to attain the political objective of war. Yet over time the definition changed. Indeed, Morgenthau (1973, p. 141) notices some alterations of the original meaning, as it shifted towards the coordination of different elements of national power, to generate the maximum effect upon those international situations which concern the national interests most directly. Hence, the original strong focus on the military aspect is no longer mentioned, though one can rightly argue that influencing the international situation also includes military aspects. A further alteration in interpretation of what is associated with a grand strategy can be detected in Kennedy's position. This author argues that one should not only include the essential political, economic, and military objects for preserving the long-term interests of a particular state but also the dynamic of balancing priorities within those interests (Kennedy 1991). Similarly, Biddle (2004, pp. 252–253) states that a grand strategy constitutes the ultimate objectives of a state by integrating military, political, and economic means to pursue its objectives within the international system.

Consequently, a grand strategy can be regarded as an organising principle for state craft: to organise national priorities hierarchically within a wider and contemporary domestic and international context to reach specific goals, which are identified of critical national interest. Therefore, a grand strategy is an articulated statement of national strategic objectives, a broad statement of strategic action, one which guides policies in pursuing and implementing those priorities and thus provides a consistent and rational framework for political decision-making over an extended period of time. As a result, a grand strategy embodies the concreteness of national politics, which may also include a geographical focus, subregional, regional or global in nature. Another crucial aspect of a grand strategy is that it will require an authoritative statement from the highest political authority, one which commands the necessary political power to implement it.

Taken together, based on the expectation that states, especially powerful ones, and strong leaders formulate and aim to pursue a coherent strategy, there should be little doubt that China and its leadership are also pursuing a grand strategy. After all, advancing concrete national, domestic, and international interests in the context of a particular geostrategic environment is not only the purpose of a grand strategy but at the core of politics as well. Yet, what is of particular interest in the context of this book is to what extent the BRI could be identified as China's new grand strategy. Addressing this question also requires an evaluation of the primary objective of the Chinese government, as this provides the genesis for formulating a grand strategy in the first place.

2.1.1   Top priorities of China's leadership

As official documentation regularly states and as China's constitution enshrines, the top priority for the Chinese leadership is the preservation of China's socialist system. Article one of chapter one of the constitution states that the People's Republic of China is a socialist state and that the socialist system represents the principal system of the People's Republic of China (Constitution of the People's Republic of China's 1999). Derived from this principle goal are specific strategies, albeit also critical; nevertheless, they have undergone alterations over time. For example, in some periods of China's more recent history, the ideological question dominated the political discourse, such as during the Cultural Revolution. Within this context, class struggle was identified as the primary task for the government and the Chinese leadership, even if developing China's economy also represented an important task. However, at the now famous Third Plenary Session of the 11th Central Committee (December 1978), class struggle was officially replaced by the development imperative. Development and the modernisation of the economy became the primary target, as generating adequate economic growth to guarantee development would have supported social stability and prosperity. Above all, though, such a strategy would have made China a powerful and respected country again (Communique 1978). It is important to remember that economic underdevelopment also carries a critical political-ideological component; an issue of which Deng Xiaoping was well aware back in 1978:

> If the rate of growth of the productive forces in a socialist country lags behind that in capitalist countries over an extended historical period, how can we talk about the superiority of the socialist system? Adding that in today's world, our country is counted as poor. Even within the third world, China still rates as relatively underdeveloped.
>
> (Deng Xiaoping, September 1978)

Moreover, economic backwardness also carried a significant nationalist aspect because, from a Chinese perspective, it deprived China of belonging to the group of leading nations. After all, restoring 'China's rightful place' among the leading nations in the world was a goal for all Chinese governments since the early 20th century, independent of their political colour.

Continuous and various official statements emphasise this enduring primacy of development for supporting China's economic enhancement. Examples include PM Zhou Rongji's 2000 Work Report (Zhou Rongji 2000), which pointed out that development is the absolute principle and the key for solving China's problems. Both the 2005 and 2012 Work Reports of PM Wen Jiabao (Wen Jiabao 2005, 2012) continued to emphasise China's persistent development challenge. In particular, the 2012 report stated that China was still facing various economic and social development challenges which needed to be addressed to enhance China's international position. This imperative is also identifiable in the repeated references to the official position that China is still at the primary stage of socialism and that it will be so for a long time to come. The announcement of the two centenary goals by Xi Jinping at the 18th National People's Congress (NPC) in 2012 also encompassed a strong development focus. While the first of those goals refers to the hundred-year anniversary of the founding of China's Communist Party in 1921, the second refers to the hundred-year anniversary of the founding of the People's Republic of China, which will be celebrated in 2049. Both anniversaries are linked with development goals. While in the first case a moderate and well-off society shall be achieved in 2021, by 2049 China will become a strong democratic, civilised, harmonious, and modern socialist country. Hence, it should come as no surprise that Xi Jinping (2018) continued to address China's ongoing development challenges in his Work Report at the 19th NPC in October 2017. Indeed, he pointed out that although a strategic opportunity for development existed, the challenges were still severe, and he added that development is the key for solving all of China's problems.

Hence, the development imperative has continued to be identified as the pivotal task for the government, not only for reaching the goal of socialist modernisation but also for China to become a prosperous and strong country once again. One resulting task is to ensure a peaceful and stable international environment, which is seen as conducive for economic development, consequently generating a critical impact on China's international politics and behaviour. Another task is to guarantee social and political stability within China – not without reason, since China's history bears many examples in which internal disunity generated considerable social, economic, and political turmoil and consequently weakened China's international positions.

However, the formulation of a grand strategy will not only reflect on the specific strategic task with which a government is confronted but will also reflect on its capabilities. This brings to the enduring discussion China's national ambitions, the impact its extraordinarily successful reform project may generate from an international perspective, and the understanding of the extent of the BRI as not only China's new-found strength but also its new grand strategy. Such an evaluation is also linked to the ongoing discussion about China being a status quo power or harbouring ambitions of becoming a revisionist state – in other words, changing from a rule follower to a rule maker, which will be evaluated in section 2.2.

2.1.2   Does the Belt and Road Initiative qualify as China's new grand strategy?

At a first glance, it seems quite appropriate to define the BRI as China's actual grand strategy, with its various regional and even geopolitical outlooks. However, after a closer investigation, such a perception can no longer be upheld, and one may consider the BRI instead as an umbrella for a range of particular policy initiatives the Chinese government is following concurrently.

At the outset, the BRI's potential for re-shaping global trade links and trade networks should not be underestimated, if it is implemented successfully. Even if the BRI was implemented partially, it could contribute to the creation of a different economic space. Depending on the extent and profundity of its implementation, this space will extend along an east-west axis from China, through Central Asia to Europe, and on a north-southwest axis from China to the ASEAN and further on to parts of South Asia. It also represents China with an opportunity of improving its bilateral relations with its neighbours and offering it an active role in different regional integration processes. This in turn may also support China's global standing and influence. Undoubtedly, the potential for creating such an alternative and coherent Eurasian geopolitical sphere is rather slim, for the time being. However, it would present an alternative to the existing geopolitical and geo-economic space, which privileges an American-European and American-Asian connectivity. Even if the BRI was implemented partially, it could herald a shift from a maritime-based network towards a continental-based one. Indeed, newly established transport links may also lead to the establishment of new economic hubs and economic corridors, which, after all, are part of the initiative. Hence, increasing connectivity between the countries of Central Asia and Southeast Asia with China may facilitate market access in both directions. Consequently, this may re-focus their economic interest, though China, as an economically stronger partner, may gain most from it. From a political perspective, China will most likely also gain political advantage from such a reorientation of bilateral cooperation and regional economic integration.

Thus, if the various BRI-related policies were implemented successfully, China would generate a multilateral framework within its periphery, one which would be shaped by its political and economic interests. This would represent a major political-economic success for China and will contribute to its domestic development and reform agenda and to the primary tasks of the Chinese government the author has previously identified. Hence, such a reading would provide a strong argument in favour of interpreting the BRI as a bold statement of China's new geopolitical strategy. Conversely, considering the various BRI-related economic initiatives and their linkage to previous and existing Chinese initiatives, such a perception may come under scrutiny. A number of specific aspects can be pointed out.

Even if China provides strong financial support for BRI-affiliated investments, the cooperation of the involved countries is a pre-request for formulating and then implementing related infrastructure projects, and of course, in the following step of forming closer trade relations. Many countries participating in the BRI are welcoming China's offer for infrastructure development. Nevertheless, they may still have different domestic priorities. In addition, once those infrastructure investments have been made, there is no guarantee for China that such links will still be used for facilitating a closer economic cooperation with China or that those countries may choose an alternative economic cooperation. Hence, many decisions with regard to the participation in the BRI and with regard to the follow-up processes are well out of Beijing's reach. This introduces considerable uncertainty in political-strategic terms for Beijing and rather undermines the argument that the BRI represents China's new grand strategy. After all, a government which formulates a grand strategy tries to ensure that it will be as much as possible in a position to implement its grand strategy. Indeed, in this regard, enough economic, political, and strategic challenges already exist at the regional and global levels.

Another aspect which undermines the argument that the BRI represents China's new grand strategy is the almost complete absence of the military dimension. No specific references are made to military strategic subjects, such as specific weapons systems, troop deployment, power projection capabilities, or war fighting doctrines. Even if contemporary concepts of a grand strategy, as the author outlined before, no longer have a very strong focus on military matters, the military aspect is not completely ignored, either. Yet any such references are complete absent in the BRI. Certainly, one could argue that, with increasing economic connectivity, close political relations follow and may result in strategic relations, which may also include strategic military topics, such as base right, which would offer China enhanced power projection capabilities. Also, one could argue that a country may not be willing to make all parts of its grand strategy public, knowing an adversary's intention is of the highest value in politics. Even so, we have to be careful of not getting carried away with speculation, either. Even more arguments undermine an interpretation that would identify the BRI as China's contemporary grand strategy, as some of its most critical foreign policy issues are not addressed in the context of the BRI. Neither China-US nor China-Japan relations nor China's role and interests on the Korean Peninsula are addressed. The failure (or one is more inclined to interpret it as a deliberate act) of not including those critical foreign policy aspects within the BRI does limit the BRI's application as China's new geopolitical strategy.

However, as mentioned earlier, a successful implementation of the BRI, or parts of it, will offer support for China's domestic development strategy and the fundamental goals associated with it. Strengthening China's regional and global position, bolstering the claim that China offers an alternative road to development, supporting domestic stability, and addressing the regional development gap within China will support the further acceptance of China's socialist system. Undoubtedly, if the BRI is successfully implemented, it will serve China's development imperative and the fundamental goals of the government quite well. In this sense, one can identify a considerable number of arguments to interpret the BRI as China's new grand strategy.

However, taking into account all of the preceding considerations, one can clearly recognise that the BRI is lacking references to several of China's most important foreign policy issues, to the geopolitical and geo-economic challenges it faces, and to the challenges related to the support of the countries participating in the BRI. The resulting picture is characterised by limitation and insecurity. Thus, one can reasonably argue that the BRI is not likely to figure as China's new grand strategy. After all, it is a rather unlikely scenario that a government will base its grand strategy on the willingness of cooperation by a diverse set of other countries and, at the same time, not include fundamental aspects of its foreign policy. Consequently, an alternative interpretation gains more value, one which interprets the BRI as an umbrella for a wide array of already existing policy strategies in which the Chinese government is interested, as well as providing new impetus for bilateral and regional cooperation.

2.2   The Belt and Road Initiative and the enduring discussion of China's international role

The debate to what extent China represents either a satisfied status quo power or a revisionist power is not a new one and dates back as far as the early 1990s, when China's economic success became internationally more visible and its economic strength increased considerably in comparison with other countries. With China's continuous economic success, the gap between the United States, the status quo power, and China also became smaller. Consequently, questions regarding its political ambitions have increasingly arisen. After all, historically, China experienced a long period of geopolitical primacy, at least within East Asia. The memory of this is still alive today, as its self-awareness as one of the world oldest civilisations clearly indicates. As such, China, its leaders, and its people hold strong self-esteem, which, in combination with increasing capabilities, may facilitate a stronger sense of 'being heard' and that its interests are 'taken into account' both at the regional and global level. As stated at the beginning of this chapter, China's reform process was extraordinary, even when it acknowledged that not all provinces could profit from it in the same way and the government is still confronted by a persisting development challenge, which will also be the focus of one of the following chapters. Yet China's economic success has contributed to its rise as a regional and global political actor by considerably increasing its political-economic relevance.

The BRI's comprehensive focus on different bilateral relationships and regional settings can be interpreted as another indication of China's new-found strength and relevance in regional and global politics. This in turn has led to a continuing speculation and strong discussion about how a rising China will fit into the existing international system and how it sees itself fitting into an international system which is based on the power and interests of the United States and a number of European countries, which are commonly described as the West. Thus, the underlying question is to what extent China will behave as a satisfied status quo power or will act as a revisionist power, by either accepting the existing international system or questioning its continuing legacy – thus being either a rule follower or rule creator. Hence, to what extent has China been socialised into established norms and pattern of interaction, based on the existing international system. This topic already represents a well-established debate, but the BRI added intensity to it.

From a domestic perspective, China's successful reform project not only carries positive economic aspects but also political-ideological and patriotic features. First of all, economic backwardness carries a noteworthy patriotic aspect. Undeniably, from a Chinese perspective, it deprived China of belonging to the group of leading nations and of its 'rightful place' among the foremost nations in the world. Indeed, restoring China to this position has been a goal for all Chinese governments since the 1911 Xinhai Revolution. As stated earlier, China's leaders and people hold strong self-esteem, and Xi Jinping's (2014) statement about the rejuvenation of the Chinese nation adds more impetus to such a perception by echoing this self-awareness. In the context of a 40-year successful reform process, it should not come as much of a surprise that we can observe a momentum of rising self-esteem among the Chinese leadership and its population. Swaine and Tellis (2000), for example, argue that a rising China will at some point result in the quest for universal acceptance of its new-found power status.

After all, during the last four decades, China's capabilities and its result-ing influence increased considerably, not only in absolute terms but also in comparison with other countries. The data in Figures 2.2, 2.3, and 2.4

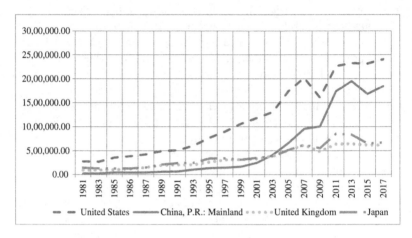

Figure 2.2 Goods, value of imports (US$ millions)
Source: Derived from International Monetary Fund data.

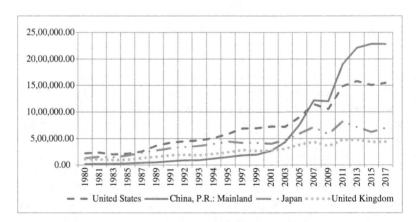

Figure 2.3 Goods, value of exports (US$ millions)
Source: Derived from International Monetary Fund data.

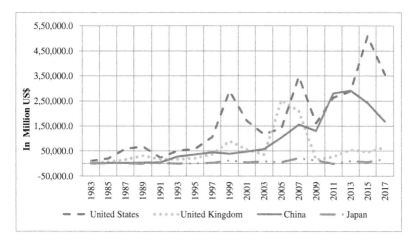

Figure 2.4 Inward FDI selected countries
Source: Derived from World Bank data.

clearly indicate China's rising economic status as it became an import partner in the international economy, for trade, and for investment.

This combination of economic success, awareness of past greatness, and increasing self-esteem is certainly not only limited to China's recent success, as we can observe such a process within most rising countries. European history and the colonial period provide extensive evidence in this regard. Yet European history and the rise of powerful states also offer ample evidence that, as a general assumption based on historical experiences, the rise of powerful states has been associated with instability and conflicts, not only within the international system but over the character of the international system itself. This leads to an associated discussion as to what extent China's rise and its integration in the existing international system will be either peaceful or accompanied by conflict, and to what extent China's rise will be associated with regional and global political-economic instability or stability.

2.2.1   Will China's rise be a different affair?

The rise of a new great power, a country that accumulates enough economic and political power to challenge the actual dominant power and has the ability of changing an existing international system, has attracted intensive discussion over millennia. This is understandable considering that the rise of a great power has, for most parts in history, led to conflicts and extensive and prolonged warfare. Reference to the rise of a new power often starts with making historical comparisons, such as the 19th-century rise of Japan or Germany and the violence this generated within the international system. Yet, the political and military conflicts associated with the rise of both Japan and Germany were unusual (this does not refer to the terrible amount of devastation they actually caused) as a dynamic and a process associated with the rise of a new great power. An extended period of conflict could also be observed when England rose to power, replacing the Spanish-Portuguese-dominated international system, and in England's competition with France over the dominant role at that time. Paul (2016) reminds us that, historically, a non-violent accommodation of a raising power was a rather uncommon occurrence and would require a mutual adaptation and acceptance by both the established and the rising power. It is therefore justifiable to ask the question: will China's rise follow those historical patterns of violent great power transformation, or will it be a more peaceful event? One associated and critical aspect remains to be considered: to what extent is China, as a rising power, willing to challenge existing institutional and power structures, which are the outcome of earlier power constellations?

First, it would be not too much of a surprise that a rising great power claimed a more active and prominent role for itself within the existing international system, as the history of the rise and fall of great powers clearly indicates. After all, the dominant power at a given period rose from a previous lower level itself because of changes in its capabilities. Ultimately, a dominant power will be challenged in time by another rising power. This in itself is not a novelty at all; indeed, it represents the core dynamic of international politics over millennia. As for China, its reform process generated an extraordinary economic success, with China becoming a leading global economic actor. Economic strength implies the quest for a stronger political role at both the regional and global levels. After all, factual power is based on economic or military strength, which still signifies an important aspect of power. Restoring China's historical foremost position within East Asia has been an important task for every Chinese government since the end of Imperial China in 1911. Xi Jinping's (2012) comments in November 2012 – 'to target the goal of a great renewal of the Chinese nation' – describing it as a celebration of its present and a declaration for the future, may be considered as a strong indication of awareness of China's own historical great power role and as a statement ensuring China's right place in the world. Taking into consideration a rather extended historical context, one could agree with Nye's (1997) characterisation that China does not represent a new rising power but rather a re-emerging power. Moreover, rising self-esteem is further enhanced when a country, as China did over the last four decades, experiences a process in which its capabilities and its power increase considerably, both in absolute terms and in comparison to other countries.

Hence, an important question arises: can we identify willingness on the side of China to undermine and eventually replace the framework and matrix of the existing international system, which was founded on the post–Second World War consensus, which is based on American dominance and the economic interests of its allies? If this is the case, it would generate destabilising effects within the international system at both the regional and global levels. Mearsheimer (2005), for example, states that China's rise will unavoidably lead to a conflict with the United States. McLauchlin (2016), instead, points out that structural change within the international system creates the possibility of conflict but does not determine it. He further argues for a shift in perspective away from focusing on power shifts and, instead, towards the threat of specific interests by either the dominant or rising power. This brings up an interesting aspect which needs to be considered, with Paul (2016) pointing out that the most critical factor for facilitating a peaceful accommodation of a rising power is linked to the willingness of the established power to pursue a strategy of gradual accommodation towards the rising power. This includes offering the status and the recognition of spheres of influence to the rising power, adding that, in the long run, accommodation may lead to the replacement of the actual power through the rising power.

China is definitely a latecomer to the liberal and multilateral global order that the United States and a small number of European states set up in the aftermath of the Second World War. However, it is worth remembering that China's successful reform process took place in the context of this US-led international liberal order and in the context of an emerging global economy. Breslin (2016) points out that China profited quite well from the existing international system and that, if China is continuing to secure access to export markets in support of its own development, it has to limit the challenge it may pose to the existing international system. Similarly, Christensen (2015) states that no other country has benefited more from the existing global order than China, since the beginning of its reform process and the related integration of its economy into the global economy. Besides, Christensen adds there is little evidence that China demands a fundamental change to organisations such as the WTO or the IMF. China not only is a member of many of the central institutions which constitute the contemporary international system (e.g. World Bank, G20, United Nations and its agencies, WTO, and IMF), but the data in Figures 2.2, 2.3, and 2.4 clearly indicate China's success within an international system which was not of its making. Such an assessment fits quite well with a repeated position the Chinese leadership has stated through the whole reform process. Indeed, stated and stated again, a peaceful and stable international environment is conductive for economic development, which will allow China to become a leading country at the global level again. However, the Chinese leadership has also ensured that China's socialist system will be preserved. Hence, as the development imperative continues to dominate China's politics, and despite all the economic success so far, China still faces a development challenge: there are fewer incentives for China to follow a strategy of undermining the contemporary international system.

When addressing the question to what extent China's rise will lead to a violent conflict situation, we may also take into consideration that some fundamental changes have occurred between previous international systems, characterised by colonial and imperialist systems and the current liberal economic one. As Ikenberry (2008) argues, the existing institutional matrix of the contemporary international system, which is structured as an open and rule-based system, and which supported China's peaceful rise, differs from that of previous historical periods when new great powers emerged. In addition, it is worth recognising that the fundamental changes which took place with regard to the global economy over the last 80 years or so, as the forceful taking of territory for increasing the economic prospect of a country, represent a lesser option in today's global economy.[1] Thus, the historical interlinked process in which a rising great power also increased its quest for territorial expansion is no longer appropriate with today's character of the global economy, since contemporary economic global integration has reached an unprecedented level that was never observed in previous historical periods. Hence, historical comparisons of great power rise may no longer offer adequate examples and may only have a limited relevance for contemporary investigations – although they should not be ignored either.

With regard to China's rise, Scott and Wilkision (2015) critically state that the 'China threat' theory has become a lens through which China's actions are generally examined, even if this too often obscures and elucidates actual developments. The authors add that their analysis of China's conduct within the WTO framework conduct offers little evidence of China being a system-challenging rising power. Indeed, China can be characterised as a rule-following and system-maintaining actor. Undeniably, over the course of the reform process, China became as integrated in the existing regional and global political and economic system as never before, since the founding of the People's Republic. This indicates China's willingness and eagerness to be a satisfied status quo power. However, as Stuenkel (2016) evaluates, rising powers such as China may still wish to establish new institutions because existing ones may be less capable of adequately integrating the interests of rising powers, even if a rising power continues to invest in existing institutions. This adds the question, what is actually on offer for a rising power such as China within the existing international order, and where in the international hierarchy should China supposedly fit in? Hence, China's support for the Shanghai Cooperation Organisation, its backing of emerging economics like the BRICS, and the initiative of founding the Asia Infrastructure Investment Bank may offer some interesting examples of strategy for a rising power. After all, these organisations improve China's position in different regional settings and also add support for its global position. However, they also address specific regional challenges and shortcomings and are also welcomed by other countries.

Another aspect which is often referred to as an indication of China's readiness to challenge the existing international system is its increasing competition with the United States. Undoubtedly China attempts to balance the US influence in international institutions, and especially at the regional level, within East Asia. Further, China has become more assertive regarding its claims in the South China Sea and in the Diaoyu/Senkaku Islands dispute with Japan.[2] Yet, Swaine and Fravel (2011) state China's greater presence and activism are, to some extent, a logical consequence of its increasing capabilities, but they wonder: does a more assertive behaviour make China a revisionist state? In their view, not really. Gilpin (1981) offers a distinctive approach in identifying between revisionist and status quo powers. Indeed, this author sustains that a revisionist country seeks to change the established distribution of power, the existing hierarchy of prestige, and the rights and rules which govern the interaction between states. Aside from this, Gilpin (1981, p. 34) suggests, other attempts of states would be rather more problematic to be interpreted as revisionist behaviour, thus a balancing strategy in international relations would not sufficiently qualify for identifying a revisionist country. Accepting such a perspective, balancing as a strategy in international relations would not be sufficiently qualified for identifying a revisionist state. Hence, China balancing against the US influence in a specific regional setting or in global organisations would not allow characterising China as a revisionist state. Johnston (2003) provides a similar argument, as balancing the influence of other powers in the context of specific issues does not in itself indicate the presence of a revisionist state. With China in mind, he argues that it neither balances as hard as it might be able to do to construct a regional anti-US alliance, especially when compared to US-Soviet competition during the Cold War period.

In the discussion on China's rise and the implications for the contemporary international system, one final relevant aspect is that the former, rather unipolar, position of the United States may not only come under challenge by China, though it may be the strongest contender. However, in a changing international system which has already become multipolar in its character, consequently weakening the former dominant position of the United States, even the United States remains the most powerful economic and military actor. Ikenberry (2014) sustains we can already observe a process of transformation within the global system. As a result, the distribution of power is shifting, as the power the United States once commanded is diffusing outward, leading to a new competition over global rule setting and institution building. Keeping in mind that the actual hegemon (i.e. the United States) is losing parts of its former strong position, we should also consider not only what some may describe as the rising competitor (i.e. China) but also the declining hegemon. After all, the rise of the new competitor occurs in a dynamic context between the established and the rising hegemon. With regard to the US position, Swaine and Tellis (2000) point out that the United States will try to arrest the gradual loss of its hegemonic position, which is taking place in the context of China's rise. In this way, they point out, the interests of the declining hegemon meet the interest of a rising power, generating a rivalry which cannot be avoided but only managed.

However, even we recognise that the international system is in a transformation process, and with it the distribution of power is changing, nonetheless the existing hierarchy within it has not yet been dissolved. Finally, we should consider Kupchan's (2014) reflection on hegemonic order: a hegemonic order also provides structuring ideas about how to rule the international system and how to organise economic and political relationships. Thus we should not perceive the American liberal world order as an expression of universal rules and ideas. After all, a rival hegemonic power will support its own cultural values and political-economic ideas. One just has to consider the characteristics and norms of the previous international system at the time of the imperialist or colonial age to recognise the value of Kupchan's position.

Notes

1 Russia's recent occupation of the Crimean Peninsula was rather based on regional and geopolitical considerations than on economic considerations.
2 However, it is important to mention that the purchase of the island by the Japanese state from the former private owner in 2012 did contribute to the escalating tensions in the territorial dispute.

3 The Belt and Road Initiative in the context of China's reform process

Addressing the challenge of domestic development by supporting transborder cooperation

Although a 40-year successful reform process transformed China into one of the leading economic powers globally, we should remember that China's development challenges continue to exist. After all, to some extent, success at the national level masks a process of inequality which occurred at the provincial level. This process of inequality is characterised by an increasing disparity in development, transcending a mere economic focus, and includes an increasing development and income gap between provinces and between urban and rural areas; the inequality of providing social welfare provisions; and different quality of education. Thus, the development gap China is experiencing transcends a narrow economic focus and points towards a wider disparity in development perspective. Furthermore, even if poverty has been reduced considerably throughout the reform period, it has not been eradicated.

Yet, some underlying aspects of this growing development imbalance were actually propelled by the dynamic of the reform process itself, as not all the provinces were allowed to participate from the beginning. In addition, geography and remoteness of western and central provinces contributed to this imbalance, as those provinces could not or only marginal profit from the sea-based global economy. Accessibility to those areas, in the form of modern transport connections, was also lacking, further undermining their attractiveness for investment. Thus, this chapter will address the topic of China's continuing domestic development challenge within the context of the BRI.

3.1 Imbalance in domestic development and the Belt and Road Initiative

One can agree with the assessment that China has transformed itself over the course of the reform period from a low-income country into an upper-middle-income country. An indication of China's development can be identified when taking into account the progress China made when applying the UN Human

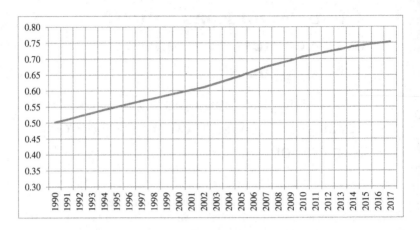

Figure 3.1 Human Development Index
Source: Derived from United Nations online data set.

Development Index (HDI). As Figure 3.1 indicates, China's HDI increased continuously in the period 1990–2017 (UN Data 2019). With a current index of 0.752, China belongs to the group of countries with 'high human development'. For comparison, OECD countries as a group attaining an HDI of 0.895 (UN Data 2019) belong to the group of countries having reached a 'very high human development'. At the same time, inequality rose as well. For example, Akhtar (2013) points out that China's Gini coefficient increased from 35 to 42 during the period 1995–2005. This observation is consistent with UN data for the period 2010–2017, which reads 42.2 (UN Data 2019).

However, to put the development success China has achieved since the reform process began into perspective, it is worth remembering Hua Guofeng's (1979, p. 21) statement in his Work Report to the Fifth NPC in 1979: 'The present level of our productive forces is very low and falls far short of the needs of the people and the country'. In addition, in his report to the 13th NPC in October 1987, former Prime Minister Zhao Ziyang (1987, p. 4) highlighted that a crucial indication of the success of the reform course was that it enabled the government to provide enough food and clothing for the overwhelming majority of China's population.

From a national level perspective, the decision which Chinese leadership made at the Third Plenary Session of the 11th Central Committee (December 1978) about focusing on economic development and modernisation to support national development and to make China a respected country again does not fit well with an increasing domestic development gap, despite its proved extraordinary success at national level. This strategic approach has not changed since then and continues to provide the political-economic framework for every Chinese government. Indeed, this development imperative is confirmed at every NPC again and again. For example, Jiang Zemin addressed it twice: first in his speech at the 15th NPC (1997), during which he stated that the leadership recognised this development challenge and, consequently, tried to reduce the existing income gaps and to minimise the regional development disparities; and second, in his address to the NPC in 2002, he pointed out that the regional development gap not only still existed but that the gap was still widening. However, he was not the only Chinese leader who was confronted by this increasing development gap. Addressing the existing development gap between the provinces was also identified as a goal in China's Harmonious Society resolution (Harmonious Society Resolution 2006). Building a harmonious society by 2020 was identified as a top political goal. Hu Jintao too, had to admit at the 17th NPC (2007) that, although the standard of living had been considerably raised on the whole, the development gap between different provinces had again continued to grow. He underlined that to address these unequal development challenges, large-scale development initiatives had to be undertaken in the western region. At the 18th NPC, Hu Jintao had to recognise that unbalanced and uncoordinated development remained a considerable challenge, although China's overall national strength had kept growing considerably and although the development gap between urban and rural areas and between provinces had become more balanced. Finally, Hu Jintao emphasised that China has to coordinate its development strategy to address this continuing regional gap (Hu Jintao 2012). Yet, based on the 2014 census, regional human development disparities among provinces remains large (China National Human Development Report 2016, p. 32). This challenge of unequal development continues today and was addressed again in Xi Jinping's report to the 19th National Congress of the Communist Party of China (October 2017). Even if he, too, pointed out that regional development had become more balanced, a firm requirement for continuing a coordinated regional development strategy and addressing inadequacies still persisted and represented an ongoing challenge for the government to address. In addition, he affirmed that China would strengthen measures to reach a new stage in the large-scale development of the western region (Xi Jinping 2018).

As the preceding statements clearly indicate, a well-established general recognition among the Chinese leadership is that the success of the reform period did not spread evenly and was accompanied with an unintended process of an increasing and persisting development gap. This matter needs to be addressed successfully, if the promises the leadership made at the beginning of the reform period are to be kept. In recognising this unbalanced regional development process as a serious development challenge for China, in 2000 the government launched the 'Go West' strategy, that is the so-called Western China Great Developmental Strategy, with a focus on developing the interior and western provinces and on reducing the existing development gap with the eastern coastal provinces. It was a much-heralded strategy to support economic development in China's remote and western regions. However, it did not lead to a process in which the western provinces would economically catch up with the more developed and prospering eastern provinces.

To some extent, this unequal development is related to the strategy of the reform process. Indeed, China's leadership initially only allowed a small number of provinces along China's east coast to be included in the reform process, even though the leadership's anticipation was that the development impulse would eventually extend to other provinces. After all, it is worth remembering a statement by Deng Xiaoping in 1990, when he discussed the introduction of market economic instruments into China's socialist economic system: 'The greatest superiority of socialism is that it enables all the people to prosper, and common prosperity is the essence of socialism. If polarization occurred, things would be different' (Deng Xiaoping 1990). Yet, such a process of development transfer from the coastal areas towards the interior and western parts of China, as the leadership assumed, only occurred partially and only over an extended period of time. This happened not only because of the unfavourable geographic locations of the interior provinces but also because of the increasing domestic competition between those provinces which had been allowed to participate from the beginning of the reform process, and consequently gained an advanced position. Indeed, during the early reform process, the restriction of economic exchange between those two categories of provinces became a familiar sign, further increasing the disadvantages of the interior provinces. Even so, the interior provinces had and have other disadvantages as well, such as an underdeveloped infrastructure, less educated work force, and a political and public administration that is less familiar with global trade. All these elements contributed to their economic disadvantage and consequently reduced their development process. This contributed to an enduring legacy of China's economic issues, characterised by a geographical inequality of development, with remote provinces and borderland areas at the lower end of the development scale.

Those differences in development experiences can also be identified in statistical data, with Xinjiang and Yunnan provinces offering a good example in this regard. First of all, Figure 3.2 indicates the ranking of these two provinces among China's provinces. Both are located at the lower end of the scale, though, and, interestingly, Yunnan ranked slightly better in the past. Figure 3.3, which compares each provincial GDP with China's average

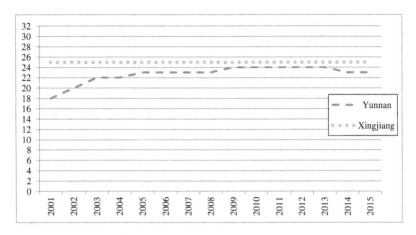

Figure 3.2 Ranking among Chinese provinces (regional GDP)

Source: Derived from various versions of Chinese Statistical Yearbook whole sample 31 provinces; Hong Kong and Macao are not included.

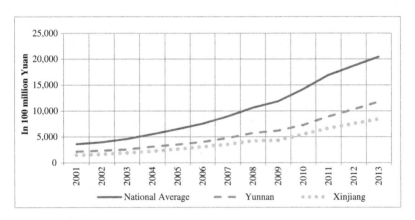

Figure 3.3 Ranking Yunnan and Xinjiang in comparison to national average regional GDP

Source: Derived from various versions of Chinese Statistical Yearbook whole sample 31 provinces; Hong Kong and Macao are not included.

provincial GDP, again highlights their rather weak position. Indeed, it also indicates that the existing gap between their provincial GDPs and the national average is increasing. Yet, Figure 3.4 illustrates per capita disposal household income, and shows an even bigger gap between provincial level

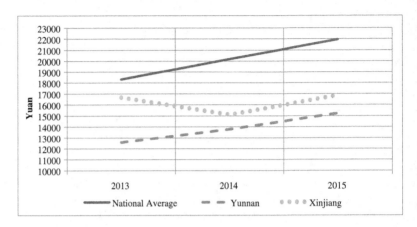

Figure 3.4 Ranking Yunnan and Xinjiang in comparison with the average provincial
level per capita disposal income of households

Source: Derived from various versions of Chinese Statistical Yearbook whole sample 31
provinces; Hong Kong and Macao are not included.

development and the national average, amid a continuous increase over the
years. Interestingly, however, Xinjiang holds a better previous position.

The BRI can be characterised as a domestic development strategy by
taking into consideration the persisting development challenge and that
the official NDRC statement of the BRI emphasises that the collaboration
between the western, central, and eastern regions should be strengthened,
for example, through the construction of specific transport corridors; the
BRI should take advantage of the vast landmass, strong industrial foundation, and rich human resources of the inland provinces (Vision and Action
2015). Hence, from a domestic political-economic perspective, the BRI has
a resemblance to a national development strategy. Indeed, both the BRI and
the 'Go West'[1] focus on a variety of provinces; yet, in both, Xinjiang and
Yunnan provinces figure prominently. Undoubtedly, the BRI implies a much
stronger international orientation but with the aim of supporting China's
domestic development by addressing the regional development gap. Within
this domestic focus, the BRI also facilitates transnational, regional, and
subregional integration processes between various Chinese provinces and
geographic areas and countries along China's international borders. Such
a transnational integration of different cross-border areas and the expected
economic development associated with it should also support the development of China's borderland areas and thus contribute to a more balanced
development within China. In this way, it will contribute to the development

strategy the leadership set out during the reform period and to the fundamental goals the government identified.

Within the framework of addressing China's development gap, as the NDRC's BRI strategy paper outlined, for example through closer cooperation between the eastern, central, and western regions, particular cities (e.g. Xian, Wuhan, Chongqing, and Chengdu) and provinces in central China (e.g. Ningxia and Gansu) will be more at the focus of development, with Xinjiang and Yunnan assuming a particular importance. Both Yunnan and Xinjiang are gaining a specific focus based on their specific geographical locations. Yunnan, for example, should further enhance its position as 'bridge' with Southeast Asia and a possible link-up with South Asia, while Xinjiang should strengthen its status as the gateway towards Central Asia and on to Europe, though it may offer a link with West Asia as well. This special support for both provinces offers a good insight in the specific nature of the BRI as a domestic-international development strategy. The following section provides a more specific evaluation of both provinces' role within the BRI framework.

3.2   The Belt and Road Initiative, support of borderland areas, and regional integration: the cases of Yunnan and Xinjiang

One official stated goal of the BRI is to support domestic efforts to address the existing development imbalance by fostering cooperation between Central, South, and Southeast Asian states and various Chinese provinces, among which Yunnan and Xinjiang are prominent. The underlying aspect is to offer support for economic development of geographically remote provinces and borderland areas, located away from the eastern seaboard, with the aim of overcoming their geographical disadvantages to the development of global maritime trade. Both provinces were rather neglected during the early phase of the reform process because they were not allowed to participate in it, while other provinces did. However, they also shared another commonality, that is geographic disadvantage and a lesser developed infrastructure connectivity.

3.2.1   *Yunnan: the Belt and Road Initiative, the Association of Southeast Asian Nations, and the Greater Mekong Subregion*

Within the strategic political-economic setting of the BRI, Yunnan's geographic location suits well for supporting an even stronger cooperation with Southeast Asia, at the regional level with the ASEAN, and at the subregional level within the GMS. Moreover, this stronger interconnectivity with Southeast Asia forms also part of China's stronger engagement with South Asia via Bangladesh and allows for closer transport interconnectivity with India. This perspective for cooperation and integration is also confirmed in the NDRC statement on the BRI by refereeing to Yunnan's geographic advantage in constructing transport corridors which will connect China with its Southeast and South Asian neighbours, as well as supporting a stronger integration within the GMS process (Vision and Action 2015).

As such, the province rises in its political relevance for the central government in Beijing and, consequently, in its political status within China. This increased political relevance of Yunnan for the centre is now commonly identifiable in the widespread description of Yunnan as a 'bridge' to Southeast Asia within the context of the BRI, thereby offering Yunnan a strategic role for increasing China-ASEAN connectivity, which would enable China to play a more active role within the GMS (Vision and Actions 2015). Such a description of Yunnan's role fits quite well with local perceptions. Summers (2012), for example, points towards a long-established discourse within Yunnan province, one which already supported a more international role of the province, especially with regard to Southeast Asia, as far back as the 1980s and 1990s. The aim was and is repositioning Yunnan from a province at China's periphery towards a centre for regional and transnational cooperation, which had official support at the provincial level. Indeed, then provincial governor He Zhiqiang stated in his 1989 Work Report that a closer cooperation with Southeast Asia had to be promoted (Summers 2012). In December 2009, Yunnan's Gateway Project was started as a direct response to the remarks then President Hu Jintao made during a visit to Yunnan in July of that year. He described Yunnan as the bridgehead towards Southeast Asia, which also supported the development of border areas and domestic connectivity (Chongui 2010). Yunnan's political-economic position was further evaluated when China's 12th Five-Year Plan (2011–2015) stated that Yunnan would be built into a bridge for 'opening up' to the southwest (China's Twelfth Five-Year Plan 2011) The State Council supported the Gateway project through a considerable investment of 500 billion yuan. With this, and further supported by the BRI, Yunnan has seen new opportunities for improving both its economy and its political standing within China's provinces. Supporting its 'bridge' functions towards Southeast Asia had become part of a national strategy for supporting a closer integration within the regional settings of Southeast and South Asia.

With regard to potential economic prospects the BRI offers, one strategy of realising these possible economic benefits for both sides can be identified in Yunnan's attempt to play a more active role within the GMS integration process.[2] Both Yunnan's provincial government and the central government expect that a stronger subregional and regional integration with Southeast Asia will lead to economic development in the province. This, in turn, will contribute to the task of addressing the development gap which exists within China. However, one contentious issue for GMS countries is the question of how to share the resources of the Lancang-Mekong river basin, which could embody potential serious obstacles for subregional cooperation within the GMS and between Yunnan and other GMS members. Besides, environmental degeneration and climate change–related risks have the potential of increasing this regional development challenge even further, consequently highlighting the political complexity of the development challenge along the Lancang-Mekong river basin and related regional integration processes. The Mekong River Commission Strategic Plan 2016–2020 identifies some of the related national strategies and challenges. Among them, there are tributary and mainstream hydropower development, expansion of irrigated agriculture, navigation, and water mismanagement (MRC Strategic Plan 2016–2020 2014, p. 7). All of those schemes are grounded in particular national development strategies but are less concerned with their potential regional implications.

When evaluating the impact and focus of the BRI with regard to Yunnan province, China-ASEAN relations cannot be ignored. Indeed, the BRI's complex character as a domestic development strategy implies a strong international focus by supporting various regional integration processes in which the Chinese government has a long-established interest. After all, China has an established record on promoting close economic and political relations with Southeast Asia and an active foreign policy towards Southeast Asia and the ASEAN over the last two decades. PM Li Keqiang, for example, expressed China's support toward Southeast Asia's regionalism by stating that China not only firmly supported ASEAN's integration and community building efforts but interpreted the ASEAN community concept as a milestone in Southeast Asia's regional integration and cooperation process. He added that China hoped to take an active part in the ASEAN Master Plan on Connectivity, with the BRI providing the framework to assist developing countries within Southeast Asia in their development (Li Keqiang 2015). In regard to the BRI, the NDRC BRI document states that established cooperation mechanisms, such as ASEAN Plus China and the GMS framework, should be utilised to support further engagement with Southeast Asia (Vision and Actions 2015).

Although infrastructure projects are currently at the forefront of cooperation of the BRI, China and ASEAN members are also focusing on the establishment of industrial zones and industrial parks to increase economic cooperation and interregional trade. This corresponds not only to the strategic outlook of the BRI but also to the strategies Chinese leadership identified at various GMS Ministerial Conferences, in which economic corridors were viewed as both linking the subregion to major regional and international markets and supporting local and subregional development (Review of configuration of the Greater Mekong Subregion economic corridors 2016, p. 1). The recently set up Lancang-Mekong Cooperation (23 March 2016) hints at a Chinese-instigated attempt for further facilitating cooperation among the Mekong riverine countries and a BRI focus on closer China-ASEAN and China-GMS cooperation. If those integration strategies are implemented successfully, they will offer additional support for Yunnan's role and its own development. Sigley (2016) describes the change Yunnan went through in the last couple of decades, changing from a backwater region into an important gateway to mainland Southeast Asia.

Yunnan's case is also strong reminder of the connection which exists between the BRI and other regional and subregional strategies of China's central government, and of how they are interconnected. As such, one could justifiably argue that China's strong political-economic interest in Southeast Asia is the driving force to include Southeast Asia in its BRI. This, once again, offers Yunnan a good opportunity for enhancing its own economic development and political prestige.

3.2.2 *Xinjiang: the Belt and Road Initiative, Central Asia, and Russia*

Regarding the case of Xinjiang, it is possible to identify a number of similar challenges Yunnan province faced in the past, such as remoteness and a 'dead-end' situation for a lengthy period of time, as the border disputes between, first, the Soviet Union and China, and, then, between the newly independent states of Central Asia and China, could not be settled within a short period of time. The question of troop deployments along the border between China and the Central Asian countries was also related to the border dispute issues. However, the actual borders in today's Central Asia have their origins at the time of Soviet Union, were drawn according to the requirement of the Soviet administration for this region and have never been meant to become international borders. It should also be remembered that additional security concerns, such as the potential support for unrest in Xinjiang, based on cultural and ethnical affiliation of Xinjiang's Uighur population with Central Asian populations, represented another security concern for the Chinese leadership. Hence, the China-Central Asia interaction developed rather slowly in the aftermath of the Soviet Union disintegration and during the early period of the reform process. Their formal diplomatic relations were established in 1992.

Xinjiang's geographical remoteness is adding to this unfavourable political situation, as the province is geographically located far away from the eastern seaboard and thus from maritime transport and the access to global trade. Another geographic feature is that huge parts of the province are desert or semi-desert areas, which also acts against being sought as a destination for economic investment. Xinjiang has a strong geographical disadvantage even within China. Taken together, these characteristics and the associated economic risks make Xinjiang a rather challenging destination for foreign investments. In order to address and reduce the development gap between the eastern coastal provinces and the inland provinces, the Western Development Strategy was created and implemented since the end of 1999. It includes Shaanxi, Gansu, Inner Mongolia, Qinghai, Ningxia, Xingjiang, Sichuan, Chongqing, Yunnan, Guizhou, Guangxi, and Tibet. Tian summarised the various aspects of China's 'Go West' strategy by listing various policy aspects, among them infrastructure investments, economic modernisation, human resource development and the promotion of science, and environmental protection (Tian 2004, p. 622). Yet as the preceding data indicate, Xinjiang could not profit extensively from the success of the reform process, either, and special economic policy strategies, such as the 'Go West' strategy, did not deliver the economic development which was expected, even though it supported local infrastructure development. Some of the aspects underlying the 'Go West' strategy of the early 2000 sound quite similar to the focus of the BRI, and, from a domestic perspective, a strong geographical overlap exists between the 'Go West' strategy and the BRI. For sure, the BRI has an added strong international focus, which was not the case with the previous 'Go West' strategy.

However, as the development gap continued to increase during the reform period, local discontent increased. During the early 1990s, according to Ferdinand (1994), the perception in Xinjiang was that Beijing was exploiting the regional resources for national development, without offering adequate compensation to the province. The long-running dispute between parts of the local Uyghur population and Han Chinese settlers, coming from the east of China, did not help either. Hao and Liu (2012) points out that one important source for discontent among the local Uyghur population is that they experience a relative deprivation, adding that the perception is that national level development programs, such as the 'Go West' strategy, will rather favour Han Chinese over other ethnic groups.

Recent and ongoing unrest within Xinjiang (e.g. large-scale riots in Urumqi on 5 July 2009); several security incidents, such as in April and June 2013, in which people and security personnel were injured or even killed; the April 2014 suicide bombing outside Urumqi's main train station; or the May 2014 bombing of an open-air market in Urumqi are all indications that a strong potential for violent unrest exists within Xinjiang. Another reason for the Chinese government to address underdevelopment within Xinjiang in a comprehensive way, hence, in the case of Xinjiang, to support regional development, also serves a political strategy. Undoubtedly, economic growth should generate local income and so contribute to social and political stability within the province. Fingar (2016) points towards this link between underdevelopment and the potential for political instability by assessing that the leadership in Beijing recognised that economic underdevelopment in border areas contributes to rising political unrest, especially within Xinjiang (Fingar 2016, p. 314).

We can observe another aspect which contributes to the central government increasing attention with regard to Xinjiang. As China's energy demand increased considerably during its reform process, the relationship with Central Asian states became an even more important topic for the central leadership in Beijing and, with it, Xinjiang's geographic location. In addressing its energy security concern, Beijing adopted a strategy of diversification, consequently opting for diversity of energy supply and supply routes. Hence, suddenly Central Asia, with its energy reserves, became an important alternative to the Persian Gulf region. This in turn also elevated Xinjiang's positions within China. The increase in trade between China and Central Asia further supported this process, and the BRI added another favourable context to it. Xinjiang now has risen in its relevance at the regional level and in geo-economic terms, being described as Beijing's gateway not only to Central Asia but also as an important section of the Eurasian continental land bridge. The NDRC's statement on the BRI refers to Xinjiang's geographic advantages in opening up deeper communication and cooperation with Central, South, and West Asia by forming a key transportation, logistic, and trade link (Vision and Action 2015).

Nonetheless, this new interest of the Chinese leadership in Central Asia came at a time when the Central Asian states looked for an alternative option to lessen their dependence on Russia. Indeed, during the Soviet period, all relevant energy export infrastructure were concentrated in one direction – towards Moscow. This legacy continued in the aftermath of the Soviet Union's dissolution, and thus offered Moscow a strong position in dealing with the newly independent countries of Central Asia. Yet, for their part, the newly independent countries were not economically able to finance the building of a new and alternative energy infrastructure which would lessen this dependence on Russia. Moreover, in the immediate aftermath of their independence, there was anticipation among the Central Asian states that Turkey, with which they had close civilisational ties, could provide the economic support they were looking for. Turkey, though, never had the economic capabilities such an engagement would require. Hence, the first agreement on a pipeline project between China and a Central Asian country, Kazakhstan, was only signed in 1997, on Kazakhstan's own initiative. However, the dynamic of cooperation between China and Central Asia changed with the beginning of the 2000s, when China became more interested in the gas and oil reserves of Central Asia for supporting its own development process and as an alternative source which does not requires to be shipped along the already choked international sea routes, such as the Malacca Strait. This also contributes to China's energy security. From a Central Asian perspective, as Peyrouse (2016, p. 216) pointed out, China's engagement offers the landlocked countries the prospect of participating in trans-Eurasian economic projects and in the global economy. As Huaheng (2016) stated, the significance of Central Asia for China's development can be summarised under the following aspects: settling border demarcation, addressing political and economic instability in Xinjiang, securing access to energy resources, and supporting local and regional trade between the Central Asian states and Xinjiang.

As for addressing the development gap between Xinjiang and China's more developed eastern provinces, it seems that further economic development in Xinjiang is closely linked with a deeper economic integration with Central Asia. Undoubtedly, a success of the China-Pakistan Economic Corridor in economic terms may also support Xinjiang's future development, even though for the time being the potential economic impact may be limited. Hence, a stronger economic engagement of China with Central Asian states not only offers interesting markets for Chinese products but also the prospect of contributing to social and political stability in Xinjiang by supporting regional development. It is important to recognise that the BRI has the potential of transcending a merely energy-related focus in China's Central Asia relations. This would take place by making another effort to stimulate local economic cooperation and trade between Xinjiang and the Central Asian countries, with the expectation that this would deliver more economic benefits to local areas within Xinjiang. Generating a stronger economic growth process and offering more economic gains to a wider section of the local population may also contribute to an easing of the ongoing social conflict we can observe. Importantly, forging closer economic relations at the regional level, between Xinjiang and the Central Asian countries, will also be beneficial to the central government strategy for securing a closer relationship with the region. However, infrastructure development still represents an important task and, at the 2016 meeting of the NPC, PM Li Keqiang reaffirmed the central government support for ongoing infrastructure development in Xinjiang (Support pledged for Xinjiang 2016). Taking advantage of the BRI and of central government support, the provincial leadership of Xinjiang stated a strategic aim is to transform

Urumqi and Kashgar into international recognised transport hubs within the context of the BRI by offering well-established connectivity hubs between China, Central Asia, and Europe (Xinjiang's Construction Plan 2017).

The announcement of the BRI, with regard to the region of Central Asia, can be interpreted as both a continuation of existing initiatives as well as a comprehensive new approach because of its enormity and comprehensiveness. This further highlights a change in the strategic perception of the Chinese government with regard to the Central Asian region and the role Xinjiang can play in this context. As the trade data in Figure 3.5 indicate, the economic relationship is on the rise, though still far beyond the level when compared with China's main trade nations (e.g. the United States and Europe), but it is still a distinctive growth trajectory since 2005 can be identified. Differently from the past, the Chinese leadership now offers a strong interest in China's relations with Central Asian countries, based on the region's energy reserves but also from a trade perspective. An additional consideration is linked with domestic politics, in supporting development in Xinjiang. Yet, China's relations with Central Asia cannot be assessed without taking Russia's interest into account, since the geopolitical dimension cannot be ignored in strengthening China's relations with Central Asia.

A strengthening of China's position in its relations with Central Asian countries will ultimately interfere with Russia's interests in Central Asia, which still perceive Central Asia as belonging to its sphere of influence. In the late 19th century and during the time of the Soviet Union, in Russia's perception, all Central Asia was an integral part of it, fully integrated into the Soviet Union's economy and political system. Certainly, human and linguistic ties between Central Asia and Russia continue to exist. In supporting

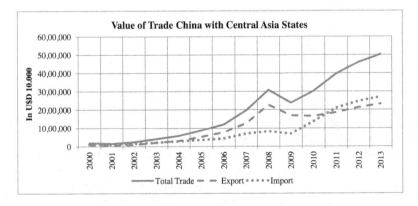

Figure 3.5 Value of trade China with central Asian states
Source: Data derived from various versions of the Chinese Statistical Yearbook.

its position within Central Asia, over time Russia has proposed a number of regional integration projects with Central Asian countries, though not always successfully. One of the most recent initiatives is the Eurasian Economic Union (EEU), which was founded in Astana in 2014, as the Eurasian integration became a geopolitical project for Russia. As any other country, Russia looks to the region's energy and mineral resources when aiming at closer economic integration with Central Asian states. As a result, as Gallo (2014) pointed out, Russia also follows a political agenda trying to balance the increasing influence of the EU and China in Central Asia.

Yet in the aftermath of the dissolution of the Soviet Union, the region definitely intended to become more independent of Russian influence, which was still strongly felt, since the entire existing infrastructure was directed towards Moscow. In addition, this infrastructure was decaying because of the economic and political challenges the newly independent states of Central Asia were facing, and the disintegration of the Soviet economy and economic space. This generated a devastating economic effect. For all these reasons, Central Asian states were exploring to develop alternative opportunities to reduce their reliance on Moscow and to get access to the global market. As a result of their own economic weakness, they were not in the position to finance new infrastructure networks themselves. However, although Russia's influence was considerably weakened, it still continued to play an important economic and political role in Central Asia.

From a Russian perspective, the EEU project may generate a dynamic within the region towards a renewed orientation to Moscow, though a regional desire to be connected with outside markets (i.e. Europe and China) continues to exist. It is possible to identify a double process of regional integration: one via the EEU towards Moscow and another via the BRI with China. However, it is necessary to ascertain how such a double process of integration will work out in economic and political terms and how the competing interests of the Central Asian countries, Moscow, and Beijing can be aligned, if they can be aligned at all. Such considerations raise the question about the compatibility of Russia's EEU and China's BRI concepts. However, when Putin and Xi Jinping met on 8 May 2015 to sign a declaration of cooperation between the EEU and the BRI, Putin stated: 'We think that the Eurasian integration project and the Silk Road Economic Belt project complement each other very harmoniously', and added that '[we] will create a common economic space across the entire Eurasian continent' (Press Statements Following Russian-Chinese Talks 2015, p. 4). Even so, one may be sceptical about the actual potential for cooperation between these two approaches to regional integration. Libman identified some of the challenges for cooperation by pointing out that both approaches have a distinctive character. Indeed, the EEU represents a regional integration agreement, which follows an EU-like model, aiming at supranational institutions and various regulatory regimes (e.g. a customs union); nothing similar exists or is planned within China's BRI (Libman 2016). From the perspective of infrastructure connectivity, both concepts offer additional capabilities with the aim of not only facilitating a closer integration between Central Asian states but also of linking it with both the European and Chinese markets.

With regard to China's BRI, Danilovich (2018) assessed Central Asia's political leaders' approach to it. In this author's analysis, they have held a quite positive view about it since the beginning, and as the cases of Kazakhstan, Kyrgyzstan, and Tajikistan highlight, there is an attempt to integrate the BRI with their domestic development strategies. With regard to Uzbekistan, Danilovich points out that the official and rather reserved discourse on the BRI changed with the death of long-time president Karimov in 2016, into a more favourable position, as Uzbekistan's current president Mirziyoyev shows a strong interest in participating in the BRI investment projects.

From a Chinese perspective, economic development and integration with Central Asian countries also hold the promise of catalysing development in Xinjiang. This supports the BRI's domestic agenda of addressing underdevelopment in remote and borderland areas. Nonetheless, even the aspect of political influence is downplayed and actually refuted in all Chinese official publications and statements which are related to the BRI. If the BRI is successfully implemented, China's position in Central Asia will be strengthened, as in other regional settings the BRI covers.

Both cases offer good insight: the BRI represents a good example of a domestic development strategy, and various aspects of its domestic focus are longer established strategies within China's reform process. Further, the BRI takes advantage of well-established foreign policy cooperation mechanisms (e.g. the China-ASEAN strategic partnership) to offer additional support for further development, both within China and in China's relations with its neighbours. Such an observation also applies to Xinjiang and its relations to Central Asian states, though, in the case of Xinjiang, addressing local security issues through development represents another important topic. From a domestic perspective, considering the overriding goal of addressing the existing imbalance and supporting the development imperative, the BRI can be characterised as another 'Go West' strategy but on a much greater scale and with an extensive international scope. When considering the BRI as a domestic development strategy, we should remember the aforementioned overall strategic guidelines for all Chinese leadership to preserve China's socialist system. Derived from this principle, goals are specific strategies, such as generating adequate economic growth to guarantee development and, with it, social stability and prosperity. Consequently, one can assess that the development imperative still dominates China's political and economic agenda. It is further worthwhile to remember that this development imperative also supports another often stated primary goal for the Chinese leadership, that China once again became a powerful and respected country. Restoring 'China's rightful place', from a Chinese perspective, among the leading nations in the world, has been a goal for all Chinese governments since the early 19th century, independent of their political colour.

Notes

1 The Western Development Strategy consists of 12 provinces, municipalities, and autonomous regions including Shaanxi, Gansu, Inner Mongolia, Qinghai, Ningxia, Xingjiang, Sichuan, Chongqing, Yunnan, Guizhou, Guangxi, and Tibet.
2 The GMS is an economic area bound together by the Lancang/Mekong River basin, which connects various parts of several countries, including China, particularly Yunnan province, parts of Myanmar, Laos, Thailand, Cambodia, and Vietnam. Nevertheless, this interest on close economic relations is not one-sided, since most ASEAN and GMS members are still confronted with underdevelopment, and good economic relations with China can contribute to their economic development.

4 Cooperation required

Reluctant partners, countries with a second thought, and disunity within the European Union

Nearly 70 countries are participating in the BRI. Nevertheless, China is still seeking more countries to be brought into cooperation with the initiative. However, successful participation depends on those countries' willingness of engagement. Although the BRI offers interesting support for infrastructure development, the prospect of economic cooperation, and the possibility of regional economic integration, participation in the BRI is not always welcomed. This is true even when infrastructure investments are required and welcome, as many developing countries are lacking the financial resources themselves. In this regard, India is a good example, as it could profit from the infrastructure investment China offers as well as from a stronger India-China economic cooperation. Yet, India's national aspirations in taking on a greater subregional and regional role support a more cautionary approach of getting deeply involved with China's BRI. Besides, India and China have not yet settled various border disputes between them, and this does not help. Another aspect seemingly rose in its recent relevance with regard to BRI-related projects. It refers to the growing economic considerations about the viability of particular projects, which are developed in the context of government changes. Good examples are offering the ongoing discussions on BRI-related projects in Sri Lanka or Malaysia. This also indicates the existence of political risks on the part of the Chinese government, when engaging with different countries.

The first section of this chapter will address India's reluctance to become too deeply involved with China's BRI. The second section will focus on countries, such as Malaysia and Sri Lanka, with previous strong commitments in joining the BRI but actually re-evaluating their commitment and considering downscaling their participation because of economic and financial evaluations.

4.1 The Belt and Road Initiative, a charming offensive which can be resisted: India, the reluctant partner

India is a good example of the challenges China's BRI may encounter, even when offering the needed infrastructure investment and potential economic advantages to its prospective partners. Indeed, so far, India has taken quite a reserved stance on China's BRI, and even refused to take part in the first BRI Forum in Beijing in April 2017, arguing that it is only an instrument for supporting China's geopolitical and geo-economic aspirations.

One may argue that India can be characterised as a special case, as it harbours its own geopolitical ambitions as a rising developing country. In this regard, India is very similar to China, at least in an abstract comparison, since India's own economic development cannot match China's development success. Even so, India not only portrays itself as the leader at the subregional level in South Asia, but it also holds wider geopolitical ambitions within Asia. India's 'Act East Policy' and its reaching out to the ASEAN, as a regional organisation, and to certain member countries (e.g. Vietnam, Thailand, Myanmar, and Indonesia in particular) clearly indicate India's ambitions. Its closer sought cooperation with the United States and Japan offers another indication of its geopolitical ambitions to further strengthen its subregional and regional position. Despite India's reaching out to other regions in Asia (e.g. Southeast and Northeast Asia), it is worth remembering that India's primary security challenges are located within South Asia. The latest bomb attack in Indian-administered Kashmir on 14 February 2019, which killed 40 Indian paramilitary police, clearly highlights this. India blamed a Pakistan-based militant group for it. In response, this led to India's air attack on Pakistan and the downing of an Indian Air Force plane, with the pilot captured by Pakistan, by the end of February 2019, though the pilot was returned to India a couple of days later. Nevertheless, this marked a major escalation between the two nuclear powers. Though the tension has been reduced for the time being, the potential for conflict and even war is quite apparent. Moreover, India's limited economic resources and strength also undermine its ambitions of taking on a greater role within Asia. Yet, as serious questions remain about India's long-term economic strength and to what extent it can afford to take on a strong position as an active actor at the regional level, Rajendram (2014, p. 3) points out that India's former 'Look East' policy has evolved into a complex strategic approach, including bilateral and multilateral levels. Under the Modi government, this policy was upgraded to what is now referred to as the 'Act East Policy'.

The state of the China-India ambivalent bilateral relationship does not help either, because it is characterised by divergent perception of each other and lack of trust. This ambivalence in their relationship manifests itself in a dynamic of regional political competition, but it certainly is influenced by the continuing dispute regarding a section of their common border. In this context, it is worth to remember China's claim to what it calls 'South Tibet', the Indian state of Arunachal Pradesh, which is located in the north-east of India. In addition, in this area, a delineated line of control which is accepted by both sides does not exist, and consequently accidental clashes between their forces on patrol are possible. However, further disagreements exist on border demarcation on other sections of their common borders. All the aforementioned circumstances and related instances have an impact on their relationship. For example, Gordon (2014, p. 139) highlights that, after the Chinese Ladakh incursion in April and May 2013, even if it only involved a small number of soldiers, India's position towards China hardened. Yet in mid-2017 another and lengthy border standoff occurred, involving military personal from both countries – the so-called Doklam crisis (June–August 2017). It was triggered by an attempt at building a road by Chinese soldiers at the Bhutan-China-India border intersection. This incidence, too, was finally solved peacefully, but it offers a viable example that the existing border issues remain a constant source of tension between India and China.

Nonetheless, the leaders of both countries are trying to control that such incidences are not getting out of hand, and are striving to form a cooperative relationship. For example, at the 9th BRICS summit (Xiamen, September 2017), the foreign secretary of India[1] pointed out that India's and China's leaders decided that the Doklam incident had to be left behind as they needed to advance their relationship (Twenty Second Report Committee on External Affairs 2018, p. 4). Similarly, the informal summit held between Indian PM Narendra Modi and Chinese President Xi Jinping in Wuhan (April 2018) provided another occasion to improve India-China relations, as they agreed that the Indian-Chinese development partnership should be further strengthened. This renewed commitment for cooperation refers to an already made commitment when President Xi Jinping visited India in September 2014 and a close partnership for supporting development was announced. Yet, Bhalla (2016) states that the existing deficit of trust in the India-China relationship generates a rather conflict-laden approach to cooperation, especially at the subregional level within South Asia. Zhongying and Sapkota (2016) concur that, at the subregional (South Asia) and regional (Asia) level, India and China are competing over spheres of influence.

However, India's more recent 'reaching out' to other regional and global partners may also be interpreted as a response to China's BRI and the related subregional inroads China made within the South Asian subregion.

In recognising China's activities in South Asia, India's foreign secretary stated that it had become a fact that China had developed strong relationships with all of their neighbours; yet, whether we treat that as a containment policy or not depends on our mindset (Twenty Second Report Committee On External Affairs 2018, p. 9). While this statement is rather more diplomatic, the wording of the external affairs committee's recommendation is rather more direct. Indeed, it stresses that China's action in South Asia indicates a deliberate policy of encirclement which can be described as containment policy from China towards India (Twenty Second Report Committee on External Affairs 2018, p. 9). Certainly, the committee supports an active policy of response on the part of India, with a focus in Southeast Asia and East Asia in exploring China's contemporary vulnerabilities, such as the territorial disputes in South China Sea, to enhance India's own position in Southeast Asia and to increase the pressure on China (Twenty Second Report Committee on External Affairs 2018, p. 9). Athwal (2008) argues that the Sino-Indian relations can be characterised as a competition in neorealist terms. Nonetheless, significant economic alterations are already taking place. Thus, it is not unreasonable to suggest that we can observe an emerging situation of economic interdependence, which may transform the existing framework of rivalry into one of cooperation. This ambivalence in the India-China relationship has become even more pronounced when considering that, at the global level and within a multilateral setting (i.e. UN, BRICS, and G20), both countries can actually work together. Thus, despite their occasionally strained bilateral relationship, we can identify the readiness for cooperation in both countries, although not without conflict.

Yet, considering these elements, India is a rather reluctant partner in China's BRI, which already provided China with an opportunity of becoming more engaged in the South Asia subregion. However, India's reluctance for cooperation with China in South Asia is also linked to its own perception of the subregional dominant power. From a strategic and security perspective, South Asia provides the most relevant focus for India's policies. Indeed, India is strategically enmeshed within the subregion, although South Asia is not of such high relevance for India's economy. Despite this, by its very size and location India is dominating the South Asian subregion, which India interprets as its own 'backyard', to use a common reference to specific interest more powerful countries may have within a specific geographical context.

From the Indian perspective, China's strong engagement with Bangladesh, Myanmar,[2] and Sri Lanka is seen as encroachment by an outsider country, a country which is not located in the South Asian subregion. Further, from an Indian angle, considerable different perceptions exist of India's role within South Asia, as well as India's own geopolitical aspirations within

Asia. In this context, it is important to notice that India and China are rapidly industrialising and ascending countries at the regional level. For the time being, though, China is far ahead in the process.

From such a perspective, India is rather cautiously welcoming China's further inroads into the subregion. After all, China already has a comprehensive and long-established relationship with India's most serious subregional adversary, Pakistan. The announcement of the recently agreed CPEC project, as part of China's BRI, further strengthens and deepens the China-Pakistan cooperation but also generates further negative responses from India. However, despite China-Pakistan relations need to be interpreted in the context of India-China relations, the relevance of China-Pakistan cooperation should be interpreted in the context that the Gwadar harbour project, which is an associated investment within CPEC, will allow China to reduce its reliance on the Malacca Strait as a major maritime route by constructing a network of road, rail, and pipeline connections with China's Xinjiang province, especially for energy shipments from the Persian Gulf. This will increase China's energy security.

As such, the 'Indian factor' may not always be as prominent in China's own decision-making as it may be interpreted in New Delhi. However, the CPEC generates some considerable backlash, because it also includes parts of Kashmir controlled by Pakistan but which is claimed by India. This in turn hardens India's stance on non-participation in the BRI. Indeed, quite strong statements are identifiable from India's side on that matter, such as that in the 22nd Committee on External Affairs report. This report states India cannot and will not accept projects which violate its sovereignty and territorial integrity, since the CPEC also includes parts of Pakistan Kashmir, which is Indian territory (Twenty Second Report Committee on External Affairs 2018, p. 11).

In this context, there are further complains from the Indian side of China's supposed insensitivity towards India's sovereignty and territorial integrity, while India accepts China's sensitivity with regards to Tibet and Taiwan (Twenty Second Report Committee on External Affairs 2018, p. 8). Yet, in easing India's concern, at least with regard to the regional implication of the CPEC, in September 2019 China and Pakistan agreed to invite third-country investors to participate in the CPEC project. Who exactly those third countries' partner will be needs to be seen; after all, the CPEC should also support local development within Pakistan.

As for the economic aspect and subregional engagement, India's own economic development still cannot draw the South Asian countries to it, as India would like to see it. Hence, for now, India's economic performance is not strong enough, and considerable doubts exist with regard to its continuing performance, especially when it is compared to China's economic accomplishments and when its investment offer to South Asia or Southeast Asia is considered. Gordon (2014) points out that India's role in South Asia and indeed its Act East Asia strategy are undermined by a lack of economic performance and domestic political instability, as they generate scepticism about India's own development and its capabilities as a regional leader and reliable partner. The lack of a strong and durable economic growth perception, which could attract the interests of India's smaller South Asian neighbours, will limit not only the economic but also the political options for India at the subregional level. Rana (2017) asserts that India's implementation record of its foreign policy is at fault, as its promises to neighbours to support and implement projects are often not hailed, or being either severely delayed, or even fail to take off at all.

This is in strong contrast with China's economic capacities and investment offers China provides within its BRI. Yet, it is not only India's economic shortcoming which undermines its leadership position within South Asia. Politics also plays an important role, especially India's self-perception as the leading power in the South Asian subregion. This perception is not necessarily shared by other countries within the subregion. Pattanaik and Behuria (2016) emphasise that India's South Asian neighbours are not at ease with India's own interpretation of being the preeminent power within South Asia, as this defies their own perception of national autonomy, independence, and state building efforts, and indicates India's hegemonic ambitions. Moreover, South Asian countries' engagement with China signifies one strategy to balance India's regional dominance. Similarly Bhalla (2016) argues that, considering the asymmetry of power between the smaller states of South Asia and India, they are forthcoming in rallying support from outside the subregion to back their interests, and thus look at China as a legitimate partner in supporting their development. However, as Yhome (2017) pointed out, India's new subregional strategy is an attempt at overcoming this long existing distrust between India and its smaller neighbours in South Asia, especially in the context of China's increasing activities within South Asia. Yet the smaller states in South Asia still detach themselves a bit from their big neighbour, an India which views itself as the successor of the British Empire in South Asia. This perception is not shared by the smaller states in the region.

From an Indian perspective, participating in China's BRI would offer China even further influence within the subregion, which, as pointed out before, is being interpreted as India's own 'backyard'. Such a consideration does not even include the strong China-Pakistan relationship, which, of course, is seen as highly problematic from an Indian perspective, to say the least. Deshmukh (2014) sustains that this reluctance continuous to exist, even if China's BRI would offer vital investment in infrastructure projects in India's underdeveloped north-eastern region. A prominent case is the BCIM-EC.

4.1.1   The case of the Bangladesh-China-India-Myanmar economic corridor

The developments surrounding the case of the BCIM-EC are a good example of the challenges, ambiguity, and strategic considerations underlying India- China relations and China's South Asian engagement, as well as the implications for the BRI.

The BCIM-EC is a major transnational and subregional policy initiative with its roots in the late 1990s and early 2000s. It represented a subregional initiative long before there were even talks on China's BRI. Within it, the concept of economic corridors is applied to support the connectivity within and between the specific geographic space and the development of remote borderland areas. Yet, as Singh (2016) reminds, India's porous north-east border with Myanmar was and still is seen as a liability rather than an opportunity within India. Consequently, this influences the domestic debate to what extent India's north-east is either a gateway or a boundary, even if the potential for positive economic development of India–Southeast Asia connectivity is widely recognised within India. In addition, it is necessary to consider the ongoing and violent conflicts between the local population and immigrants from other parts of India to the north-east, and a related long-running insurgency based on ethnic lines.

Even so, there was a period where the outlook of supporting the implementation of the BCIM-EC became rather optimistic. It was not before the 2013 visit of China's PM Li Keqiang to India, during which India and China established a joint study group. This offered a strong official endorsement of the BCIM-EC proposal. Some progress has taken place within the BCIM-EC framework, such as the various meetings of the Joint Study Groups (2013/2014/2015) on strengthening connectivity within the subregion. After all, the potential for supporting subregional economic development is apparent. Indeed, implementing the BCIM-EC would offer an increasing interconnectivity within the South Asia subregion but also an increasing connectivity between South Asia and Southeast Asia, and with it the potential of economic growth and development. Furthermore, in extension via Southeast Asia, interconnectivity with China will also be gained. From an historical perspective, the BCIM-EC is to revive parts of the so-called ancient Southern Silk Road, which once connected south-west China with Southeast Asia and South Asia.

With regard to the potential for local development, Yhome (2019) stresses that, even if the area the BCIM-EC covers is characterised by poor infrastructure, it is rich in natural resources and thus holds considerable potential for supporting development. Also, the BCIM-EC would fit well with India's own 'Act East Policy' and its strategic courting of ASEAN. Thus, this will generate economic growth in India's underdeveloped north-east. Nag (2016, p. 145) states that for India's Act East Policy to be implemented successfully, achieving greater physical connectivity between India and Southeast Asia is an essential requirement. Assam's Chief Minister Sonowal (2017) emphasises that a long-term goal is to develop a comprehensive infrastructure connection with the ASEAN countries and with China to become embedded in trans-Asian infrastructure networks. In addition, another aim is to build and industrial corridor within Assam.

There seems to exist a strong economic rationale for India to participate in such China-led infrastructure projects in its north-east to establish infrastructure connectivity with Southeast Asia and in extension with China. However, we should keep in mind that the situation may be viewed differently from a security perspective. Undoubtedly, the BMCI-EC has offered the required infrastructure investment and the prospect for economic growth for an underdeveloped area within India. Nevertheless, the BMCI-EC process rather stalled over time because of geopolitical considerations on the part of India. China's move to integrate the BCIM-EC into the BRI does not help, either, at least from India's perspective, because it may be perceived as another step of a strategic action in encircling India in its own subregion. However, from a Chinese perspective, it makes sense to integrate different major subregional integration processes into one strategic framework. Yhome supports this position and stresses that the BCIM-EC has been originally interpreted as a stand-alone project with a sole focus on supporting development within a particular geographic area. This interpretation changes with the announcement of China's BRI, as BCIM-EC is now interpreted as part of a wider strategic framework (Yhome 2019). In this changed context, various critical aspects within the BCIM-EC framework are increasingly aired by Indian analysts. Sajjanhar offers a good overview of these aspects by pointing out that it will be China which will not only profit most economically with the prospect of bringing India's north-east under increasing Chinese influence, but China will also gain strategically by getting a direct overland access to the Bay of Bengal (Sajjanhar 2016, p. 4). Thus, such consideration does not play down well from an Indian perspective, to say the least.

Since such considerations are not a single opinion from an Indian perspective, it should no longer come as a surprise that, as Karim and Islam (2018, p. 285) state, it is to India's reluctance that within the BCIM-EC approach the intergovernmental level has not been institutionalised, so far. Rana (2017) stresses that India views China's proposed investments in the north-east in the context of the continuing border disputes with China in that area and a prevailing opinion of rejecting Chinese investment offers among Indian policymakers. Even so, it would be worthwhile to take a selective approach in considering some investment offers, not least as investments from other paths of India into the north-east are quite low. Deshmukh (2014, p. 26) points towards potential implications of the lack of India's BRI engagement since India's neighbours have already committed to participate in it. Hence, Indian reluctance of doing so not only increases the pressure it faced at the regional level, but it may also miss an opportunity of gaining domestic economic benefits. This, in turn, may undermine India's position within South Asia but may also deprive it of closer cooperation with Southeast Asia because of missing infrastructure interconnectivity. After all, China's BRI could offer some critical infrastructure investment in north-east India, which indeed could facilitate a closer India-ASEAN economic integration, as well.

Thus, India's response offers a viable example of how geopolitical complexity at the regional level can undermine local and subregional approaches for cooperation and the ability of generating development support. Karim and Islam (2018, p. 297) affirm that even if India was originally supportive of the BCIM-EC strategy, over time it seems it has become too much concerned with the project. India tends to adjourn subregional integration dynamics within South Asia of not undermining its own regional political and economic dominance. However, Rajendram (2014, p. 9) argues that China's quite successful engagement with South Asian countries represents another dimension of India's own strong focus on East Asia, which one could almost interpret as a countermove. An alternative proposal from an Indian perspective exists and would also facilitate its 'Act East Policy' and its ambition of closer cooperation with the ASEAN: the India-Myanmar-Thailand Highway project. In the end, this connection would also link up India with southern China via the GMS-China infrastructure projects, though the distance from south-west China to the South Asian subregion, and thus to India, would be considerably greater. However, India's reluctance to join China's BRI offers a good example of the challenges China can encounter, even though it offers its prospective partners considerable infrastructure and potential economic advantages.

4.2   Countries with a second thought

In recent times, a number of politicians and economists in different countries that once courted Chinese investments have publicly expressed concerns that some of the projects are too costly and could generate too much debt for them. Hence, the concern about economic viability of some BRI-related projects has increased. This renewed attention to the associated costs with BRI-related projects mostly occurs in countries along the Indian Ocean shoreline, an area where an ongoing and strong regional competition exists between China and India and have arisen in almost all the cases with a change of government in those countries.

4.2.1 Malaysia

With a change of government in Malaysia, after a shock defeat of then PM Najib Razak in the general elections of May 2018, Malaysia's old strongman and previous PM Mahathir became PM again and suspended several China-related investment projects. These include the East Coast Rail Link and two pipeline projects – all are important projects within China's BRI with a combined value of about $23 billion. The foremost argument for this change of mind of the new Malaysian government is based on its assessment that the previous Najib Razak government had accumulated an extraordinary budget deficit, which needs to be reduced urgently. As such, the hold of the implementation of the projects and the attempts of re-negotiating the related costs are not an indication of the new government's different attitude to China-supported infrastructure investment. After some confusing reports and statements about the status of the East Coast Rail Link project during March 2019, a renegotiation process regarding its costs is underway. The actual situation in mid-April 2019 seems that the East Coast Rail Link is back on track, partly re-routed and with reduced length to 648 km, which is 40 km less than the previously planned length, though it still will reach Port Klang on the Strait of Malacca. It was further announced that an agreement between China and Malaysia had been reached in continuing the projects, though at a lower cost, reducing the price tag from 65.5 billion ringgits to 44 billion ringgits. In addition, there are also indications that the local contribution to the project will be raised as well.

The renegotiation of the investment project took place at government levels, which should not be surprising, considering the importance of the issue to the Malaysian and Chinese governments. However, it does not seem that Malaysian-Chinese relations will touch the bottom. Earlier made statements by PM Mahathir in early March 2019 support such an interpretation, that the re-evaluation of China's infrastructure projects is not an indication of a fundamental change in Malaya-Chinese bilateral relations. PM Mahathir stated that China's investment is still very welcome in Malaysia, but it should support employment within Malaysia. He further assessed that China's BRI is not related to an attempt by China to increase its dominance or empire building, even though he recognised that China, as an emerging powerful country, aims to increase its influence. Although Malaysia and

China have been neighbours for 2,000 years, China has never conquered Malaysia, in contrast to the Europeans, who conquered Malaysia within two years of their arrival, in 1509 (Mahathir 2019c). Indeed, as he pointed out on various occasion, PM Mahathir emphasised that not only does Malaysia still highly value its relations with China, but that he himself already stated in the past that he supports the BRI (Mahathir 2019b). In an earlier interview, PM Mahathir alleged that China's government understands the serious financial situation Malaysia is facing, and that it has accepted that Malaysia has to reduce its financial debts (Mahathir 2019a).

That Malaysia's new government decision to re-evaluate China's infrastructure projects is based on financial and economic considerations and not on a sharp turn in their bilateral relations is supported by the Malaysian government's postponement of another important infrastructure project – the Malaysian-Singapore high-speed railway link – which should connect Singapore with Kuala Lumpur. Again, as is the case with the Chinese-supported infrastructure projects, this project has not been cancelled but has been postponed until May 2020.

4.2.2   Sri Lanka

Hence, it now becomes a quite familiar affair of speaking of being lured into a Chinese debt trap, as China is offering easy acceptable loans as part of its BRI, with Sri Lanka presented as a primary example. The close cooperation between the previous Sri Lanka President Rajapaksa with China was sometimes described as 'Colombo Consensus', and it would not be wrong to point out that the initiative came from the Sri Lankan side. Yet the development of this close cooperation had to be seen in the context of how the decade-long Sri Lankan civil war ended. Indeed, in the final months of the civil war in 2009, grave human rights violation and war crimes took place. The government forces were accused of indiscriminate shelling of fighters and civilians, which led to the death of tens of thousands of people. This generated considerable international criticism from many countries and a UN investigation into such claims, with the Rajapaksa government refusing cooperation with the UN.

In that situation, and in dire need for financial sources for rebuilding the war-devasted country, China, which is known for its stance of not getting involved in domestic politics and of not attaching any political demands to its lending, was welcomed as an important investor and ally. Thus, China became a source for additional funds, also to finance local projects, even if they carried potential geopolitical implications, transcending mere national Sri Lankan considerations. The Sri Lankan-Chinese projects, which became rather more controversial over time, are Hambantota port, Colombo port city, and the Matalla airport. The first two projects became also quite notice-able projects in China's BRI.

As Sri Lanka has a prominent location along important global shipping lines, China's investment has become an important topic in geopolitical terms, and not only one considering India's cautions of China's investment activities in South Asia. We should keep this in mind when following the discussion and evaluation of China's Sri Lanka involvement. Even so, this should in no way neglect Sri Lankan domestic aspects of China's investment and the implication of it. For example, in January 2017, violent opposition and protest erupted because of an industrial zone project China supported and related to the Hambantota port project. The Sri Lankan government finally approved the go-ahead of the industrial zone project in June 2018. However, the episode offers an insight into the potential of conflicts with which China's overseas investment may be confronted. Such protest has characterised many World Bank, ADB, and other donor projects, and certainly these are not solely related to China's BRI. Even so, instances of local dispute should not be ignored either.

The recent headline-gripping aspect of BRI-related investments in Sri Lanka, the Sri Lankan government amassing financial debt, and the potential political implication this may generate allow to identify critical voices. Weerakoon and Jayasuriya (2019) disagree with such a narrative and with the 99-year lease of the strategically important Hambantota port quoted as the prime example. They argue that Sri Lanka's financial problems, the very possibility of default, and its repayment problems have very little to do with Chinese loans, as they only constitute about 10 percent of its total foreign debt. According to Weerakoon and Jayasuriya, making the decision to lease Hambantota port to China was part of a strategy of generating cash to increase Sri Lanka's national reserve funds, and not to pay back Chinese debts. Esteban (2018) argues in a similar way, pointing out that, as Sri Lanka has accumulated a public debt of 77 percent of its GDP, its debt problem extends beyond its commitment to China. Based on the Central Bank of Sri Lanka's annual report, the ownership of outstanding foreign debt shows a different picture. The leading lenders of money by far, on a multilateral basis, are the ADB and the World Bank's International Development Association. The three leading countries lending to Sri Lanka, in the bilateral category, are Japan, India, and China. Japan owns considerably more than either India or China. However, all of them are dwarfed by the amount of money the Sri Lankan state owes to the financial markets through commercial lenders. As Weerakoon and Jayasuriya (2019) pointed out in their assessment, the reason why Sri Lanka is so widely portrayed as an example of the dangers of Chinese debt diplomacy, although Chinese loans are not the primary cause of Sri Lanka's debt problems, is linked to global politics

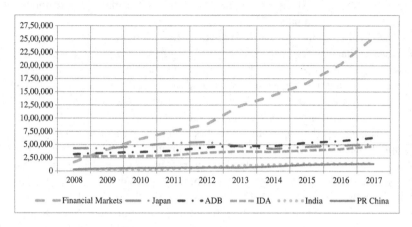

Figure 4.1 Sri Lanka outstanding debt (Rs million)

Source: Compiled from the Central Bank of Sri Lanka Annual Report 2018 (2017 data are provisional).

rather than to the real facts of the Sri Lankan case. Based on the following data from the Sri Lanka's Central Bank (Figure 4.1), Weerakoon and Jaya-suriya's assessment needs consideration.

Financing the port development increased Sri Lankan national debt and led to some local demonstration over the associated land-lease agreements. Yet as the example of the rapid construction of the Port of Colombo container terminal indicates, financing the port enhancement considerably increased the capacity of the Port of Colombo. This can support economic development. Undoubtedly, we still have to wait before we can assess the economic impact BRI-related investments have on Sri Lanka's further development and with it, the controversy of foreign, and especially Chinese, investment will continue.

4.3   The European Union, a partner plagued with internal disunity

When considering EU's involvement in China's BRI, it is plausible to characterise it as plagued by internal disunity. While a number of Central Eastern European states, such as Poland, the Czech Republic, Slovakia, Bulgaria, and Serbia (which is not a EU member to date), are quite interested in participating in China's BRI to upgrade their own infrastructure, the leading economic countries within the EU have become a bit more sceptical about a too deep cooperation. As to China, it is quite forthcoming in supporting those Central Eastern states in their participation in the BRI. Also, the 16+1 framework[3] has become the signpost for it, as it supports a stronger China's engagement with several European states.

Certainly, improving the infrastructure in those countries will reduce the transport time for Chinese goods to be sent to Europe and support a closer economic cooperation between those countries and China, but it will also contribute to national level infrastructure development as well as EU's wide infrastructure integration. Hence, for all these reasons, the leaders of these countries are quite supportive to China's BRI. Polish President Andrzej Duda, for instance, expressed his country's interest in strengthening Polish-Chinese cooperation through various BRI-based projects. Duda praised the BRI as a significant contribution to a more balanced and sustainable development of the global economy (China, Poland Urged to Seize Opportunities 2017). Similarly, Serbian PM Ana Brnabić has pointed out that China's BRI not only supports infrastructure development, such as road and bridge building in Serbia, but it also helps to create employment in Serbia, adding that Serbia's citizens already recognise the positive results from the BRI (Belt and Road Initiative Boosts Development in Serbia: PM 2018). Yet, from an EU perspective, it will increase the infrastructure connectivity between the newer Central and Eastern European members and the older member states, and it will link to the Central Asian countries as well. Indeed, the BRI's potential contribution to economic and political stability in Central Asia may also offer stronger economic opportunities for European countries.

At the same time, the 16+1 framework has also generated some reservations within the EU, as it targets particular member countries. Indeed, China's BRI may offer China increasing economic and political leverage in these countries and a bridgehead into the European market and in influencing European affairs. An EU Parliament Briefing points towards such a perception, stating that one of the main issues with the 16+1 format is how it will impact on the EU internal political dynamic and the EU's political unity. The document adds that for China it represents an attractive strategy, as it provides China with a strong platform to advocate its BRI (China, the 16+1 Format and the EU 2018, 2, 3). With the founding of the EU-China Connectivity Platform in September 2015, some concern related to the 16+1 framework may be addressed by generating an EU-wide focus for China's infrastructure investment in the EU. At the 3rd Chair Meeting of the EU-China Connectivity Platform, it was emphasised that the synergies between China's BRI and the EU's Trans-European Transport Networks should be strengthened and that infrastructure connectivity represents a priority for EU-China relations and cooperation (3rd Chairs Meetings 2018). This position was confirmed at the 4th Chair Meeting, in April 2019 (4th Chair Meeting 2019). However, continuing Chinese investment and especially acquisitions of high-tech companies in Germany have led to increasing scrutiny of such deals at both the national and EU level, as the concern to protect Europe's technological advantage increased. Yet, in early March 2019, Italy announced its willingness to become a strong partner in China's BRI. This ambivalence can also be identified at the EU level, as in March 2019 the EU Commission pointed out that China is both a cooperation partner and an economic competitor, adding that China also represents a systemic contender, since it offers an alternative governance model (European Commission 2019a). This topic also dominated the most recent EU-China Summit meeting, in April 2019. The related press statement of the European Commission states that, while China's economic strength and political influence make it an essential partner for the EU and vice versa, the balance in the relationship has shifted in favour of China, especially in economic terms (European Commission 2019b). Even so, the summit joint statement states that the EU and China reaffirm the strength of their Comprehensive Strategic Partnership, adding that two sides will continue to identify synergies between the EU's strategy on connecting Europe and Asia, the Trans-European Transport Networks, and China's BRI (European Council 2019).

Notes

1 The foreign secretary is the administrative head of the Ministry of Foreign Affairs of India.
2 Even if Myanmar is an ASEAN member and is linked with the Southeast Asian subregion, in the discussion about China-India relations and India's considerations of China's action within South Asia, it needs to be considered in the South Asian context as well.
3 This is cooperation between China and a number of Central and Eastern European countries, currently numbering 16: Albania, Bosnia and Herzegovina, Bulgaria, Croatia, the Czech Republic, Estonia, Hungary, Latvia, Lithuania, Macedonia, Montenegro, Poland, Romania, Serbia, Slovakia, and Slovenia.

5 Regionalism, regionalisation, and the Belt and Road Initiative

As the persistent relevance of regions in international politics is identifiable from a theoretical and practical political perspective, the issue arises to what extent China's BRI fits with the character of contemporary regional integration processes. Such considerations are also linked to the ongoing discussion related to the changing nature of regional integration processes. They can be differentiated between regionalism processes, which are defined as state-led, so-called top-down processes, and regionalisation processes, which are characterised by local and non-state actor integration initiatives and are defined as bottom-up processes. With contemporary regional integration processes characterised as bottom-up processes, the question arises to what extent the BRI would fit into which category, not least because of the economic and geographic scale covered by the BRI. Thus, the question arises to what extent we are witnessing the return of regionalism and a waning role of regionalisation, which for a considerable time had rather dominated contemporary integration processes. In addressing this topic, we first have to identify the differences between regionalism and regionalisation in more detail.

5.1 Regionalism versus regionalisation

An established characterisation of regional integration processes differentiates between top-down and bottom-up processes as a cause for regional integration processes. While 'top down' refers to a process of regional integration in which states are the leading actors, with a clear focus on the integration of national economic spaces through the creation of regional institutions such as the EU, 'bottom-up' processes refer to local and subnational level actor involvement in taking the lead in facilitating regional integration processes. Bottom-up regional integration processes are also characterised by less formal institutional integration. From an historical perspective, another distinction is made between the so-called first wave and second wave regionalism. 'First wave' regionalism refers to the regional integration processes which took place between the aftermath of the Second World War and the early 1970s, and which were mostly characterised as state-led projects. 'Second wave' regionalism originated from the middle of the 1980s onward and is characterised by local inspired cooperation based on geographical proximity and the prospect of generating local gains. Examples include growth triangles (e.g. the Indonesia-Malaysia-Singapore Growth Triangle) or subregional cooperation processes, such as within the Danube and Mekong River basins. Thus, the focus of second wave regionalism is on generating a positive economic and development impact at the local level but within a wider geographical context, often transcending a single national economic space.

When identifying the differences between first wave and second wave, or 'old' and 'new' regionalism as they are also sometimes labelled, we also have to take into account the fundamental challenges which have occurred at the global level. The most consequential one was the end of the Cold War period and, with it, the end of the associated superpower competition between the United States and the Soviet Union. This led to a transformation of the international system from a bipolar to a multipolar system, consequently opening up political space and stimulating regional integration processes, thereby generating new economic space by transcending previously impregnable borders.[1] Examples are the subregional economic integration processes along the Danube basin in Central and Eastern Europe or the integration dynamic with the GMS. Neither of them would have been possible during the Cold War period, as the then existing political division cut through those international river basins. Hence, the political effect which was associated with end of the Cold War period generated a positive effect on regional integration dynamics, which can be observed empirically, as a new resurgence of regionalism since the late 1980s in world politics is observable. This impact of a systemic change at the global level is identified in various academic assessments, such as Telo's (2014, p. 6) widely shared assumption that the end of the Cold War strengthened the tendency towards a plurality of international actors, notably states and regions. Hettn, Sunkel and Inotai (2001, p. 33) also underline that not only is a genuine worldwide phenomenon taking place, since regionalist dynamics are observable in more areas of the world than ever before, but it is also characterised by a complex process which concurrently involves states and non-state actors alike.

Another almost equal relevant structural change occurred at the global level. It is related to an increasing global economic interconnectivity, which is described as the process of globalisation. Indeed, the globalisation of economic activities (e.g. the creation of international production networks, an accompanied revolution in transport, and the consequent shrinking of space) contributed to a different structural global economic environment which stimulated regional processes, that is 'second wave' or 'new' regionalism. However, the author of this book does not agree with the argument that globalisation has generated a 'borderless economy' in which states have been replaced by markets, as Ohmae (1990) sustains. Instead, the author would rather support Scholte's (1997) evaluation, because he offers three common understandings of globalisation: one identifies globalisation as an increase of cross-border relations; another treats globalisation as an increase of open border relations; the third regards globalisation as an increase of transborder relations (Scholte 1997, pp. 430–431). A globalising economy, which is characterised by global production chains taking advantage of local specific advantages, such as lower production costs in combination with reduced transport costs, has also supported a regional and subregional integration dynamic, often focusing on the potential gains at the local level. This in turn supports a bottom-up dynamic of regional integration.

As a result, we have to recognise that contemporary regional integration processes, whether occurring at the national or subregional level, are taking place in the context of a different global structural environment, which considerably differs from first 'old' or 'first wave' regionalisation processes. Further, within 'new' or 'second wave' regional integration processes, local support for integration often takes on a critical aspect. In recognising these differences, a new differentiation has been made, instead of speaking of 'old' versus 'new' or 'first wave' and 'second wave' integration processes, which differentiate between regionalism and regionalisation. Addressing the differences between regionalism and regionalisation, Breslin and Hook (2002, p. 4) state that regionalism refers to the conscious, deliberate, and purposive attempts national states make to create formal mechanisms, consequently representing a top-down integration process, whereas regionalisation characterises a bottom-up process, which is informed by the actions of non-state actors based on economic incentives. Similarly, Hettn, Sunkel and Inotai (2001) state that regionalism is generally associated with a deliberate strategy of a national actor and involves formal institution building, while regionalisation stands for a processual dynamic based on the pattern of cooperation and integration within a particular cross-national space below the national level.

As contemporary regional integration processes are commonly described as bottom-up integration processes, the question arises to what extent the BRI would fit into such a description not least because of its economic and geographic scale. Indeed, does the BRI present a challenge to the prevalence of so-called bottom-up integration processes? Hence, does the BRI indicate a return of regionalism?

5.2   The Belt and Road Initiative, a return of regionalism

It is rather hard to miss the top-down character of the BRI. First of all, its origin is widely attributed to two statements President Xi Jinping made on overseas visits. One statement relates to a state visit to Kazakhstan (September 2013) to propose the Silk Road Economic Belt, along the historical Silk Road from China through Central Asia to Europe. The other statement was delivered in a speech at the Indonesian Parliament (October 2013) and proposed a maritime version of the ancient Silk Road, the 21st-Century Maritime Silk Road. However, the top-down character of the BRI is not limited to its inauguration by President Xi Jinping but indeed represents its general character, as the process is based on state-to-state cooperation, with relevant decisions being made between China's government and other governments, even though the actual implementation of investment projects will be based on company levels. In addition, China's official statements about the BRI (e.g. the NDRC's account on the BRI) also emphasise that closer state-to-state economic relations with other countries should be achieved through a successful cooperation through the BRI and by facilitating existing cooperation with regional institutions (Vision and Actions 2015). Indeed, a special emphasis is oriented towards existing cooperation with regional organisations, such as the Shanghai Cooperation Organisation, the GMS, the ASEAN, or the EU (Vision and Action 2015). These regional organisations can be characterised as state-led regional organisation supporting a state-led integration process within their individual region. An example can be the fundamental principles underlying the ASEAN cooperation, as outlined in the Treaty of Amity and Cooperation in Southeast Asia, which refers to mutual respect for sovereignty, independence, and territorial integrity of all nations. Another example is the Shanghai Cooperation Organisation, whose strong state focus is identifiable in its organisational structure. It is headed by the 'Council of Heads of States' and the 'Council of Heads of Government', where the PM of the member states meet; this highlights its strong state focus. In addition, other country-to-country level cooperation and cooperation such as the Central and Eastern European 16+1 forum are within the focus of the BRI. Likewise, the strategic approach of enhancing policy and intergovernmental coordination among the BRI countries (Vision and Action 2015) refers to the national level as the central focus for cooperation. The same does the Joint Communique which was issued at the end of the Second Belt and Road Forum for International Cooperation, held in April 2018 in Beijing. Indeed, the Joint Communique refers to the Leader's Roundtable as the source of formulating and agreeing on the Joint Communique as well as references made within it, which too refer to states as the partners within the BRI process, and for respecting the sovereignty and territorial integrity of the participating states (Joint Communique 2019). Thus all of these features and statements support a characterisation of the BRI as a top-down and state-led regional integration process.

In addition, the BRI should also take advantage of and support China's foreign policy strategies, such as its common use of Free Trade Agreements, which, of course, is another state-led process. Another example is China's engagement with Southeast Asia, which is based on two principle levels: on a regional level, via China-ASEAN relations, and on state-to-state level, between China and the various Southeast Asian countries. A comparable situation can be identified with China's BRI engagement in general, as the BRI cooperation, wherever it takes place, in Central Asia or with European countries, is at state-to-state level. Another stated aim of the BRI is related to another state level policy, to support and further advance China's periphery diplomacy in enhancing its neighbourhood relations. Another common description of the BRI defines it as a new form for regional cooperation and integration, with repeated recurrence to the argument that it will lead to a 'community of common interests' and 'common destiny' among the participating countries. Once again, the link to the state level is made. Yet, such a perspective of close cooperation for different countries also represents the core aspect of regionalism, though, from a theoretical perspective of regional integration, the BRI does not pay too much attention to institutional building, as it is usually the case with state-led integration processes. Nevertheless, repeated references are made to a future closer economic cooperation and integration among the participating countries. However, the BRI's scale is unique in terms of the geographic area and people it covers. Another hint that the BRI confirms to be a 'state-led' integration process can be identified in the repeated statement of the Chinese government that cooperation is based on the preparedness of other countries to participate. Once again, the state-to-state level becomes obvious. Thus, from an analytical perspective, China's BRI can be characterised as regionalism, that is, as a top-down project.

This strong and continuous reference to the state as the main actor in supporting international cooperation and development relates to China's own development experience, in which the state has played a crucial role. The term 'Beijing Consensus' refers to the political-economic strategy of China's reform period. In this strategy, the state takes on the leading role in development; as such, it depicts a difference to the market-led model of development, which is often described as the 'Washington Consensus'. Thus the emphasis is on a strong state-led transformation process, top down in its character, while policies that are associated with the Washington consensus rather support bottom-up policy dynamics. It is further worth remembering that many cooperation partners in the BRI can be characterised as rather strong centralised countries with less developed federal systems, which also supports a national level analysis within the context of the BRI. Indeed, with some respect, China's own provincial governments may even taking on a more political and economic relevant role as other territorial units do in many of China's BRI cooperation partners.

At the same time, importantly, although we can characterise the BRI as regionalism, for the time being it does not support such a strong economic integration process as associated with regionalism, such as the building of a common market. However, China's official statements related to the BRI regularly state that supporting a closer economic cooperation and integration is also part of the BRI process, but to date it has not really materialised. Thus a primary aspect of a regionalist integration process is missing to date, although it may emerge in the future. This, of course, depends on the success of the initial BRI-related investment projects. Even so, the BRI clearly indicates that the state has a continuous role to play in facilitating regional integration dynamics and processes and in supporting development. As for its actual relevance as a regional integration model, there should be no misunderstanding in recognising that, if the BRI is implemented successfully, even only partially, it could create a dynamic which may lead to a new economic space which will extend along an east-west direction from China through Central Asia to the EU, and in a north-south-west direction from China to the ASEAN states and further on to parts of South Asia. Such a development would raise additional geopolitical and geo-economic issues, as it could lead to a shift in the global economy, both from a geographical perspective and for the actors involved. The NDRC statement on the 'Belt and Road Initiative' also emphasises that the BRI facilitates the trend towards a multipolar world and economic globalisation by promoting comprehensive development of bilateral relationships (Vision and Actions 2015). A final aspect associated with the BRI is it reminds us of the continuous significance of geography even if we are living in a supposed globalised world.

Note

1 However, it should also be mentioned that, at the same time, the removal of this great power overlay also led to an increase of regional instability and conflicts. The rise in local and regional conflicts all over the world, including Europe, is a reminder of the other impact the end of the great power competition had, as it allowed local- and regional-inspired conflicts to spread.

6 Conclusion

6.1 The Belt and Road Initiative: a complex developmental strategy

Even as the BRI calls on an association with the historical Silk Road, the comprehensive geographic scope, the great number of different countries within various regional settings, adds to its complexity and to a conceptual challenge as the BRI is characterised by a combination of a domestic and international development strategy. An aspect often overlooked in the international discussion about the BRI's character is its domestic focus seen from a Chinese perspective. Indeed, the BRI aims to address ongoing developmental challenges that China is still facing, despite the extraordinary success of its reform process. Though it is unquestionable, that BRI does have an international focus as well.

From a regional perspective, the BRI's potential impact can be related to Central Asia, Southeast Asia, and South Asia by offering various incentives for economic and political cooperation and integration within these different regional settings, although cooperation with the BRI is required to generate such a positive impact for regional integration, but cooperation is not always granted. After all, cooperation from other countries is essential for the success of the BRI in general and the potential impact it may generate. However, not all countries are happy to be getting involved in China's BRI, even though participating countries would profit from the infrastructure investment offered.

India's reluctance to participate offers an excellent example. To be frank, one can identify a good number of arguments – from an Indian perspective – for its reluctant behaviour. For instance, India has its own national strategy which focuses on deeper political and economic integration in East Asia; supports the so-called Act East policy; and favours Japanese PM Shinzo Abe's Indio-Pacific strategy. That strategy aims to create a different perception within East Asia and a stronger inclusion of the United States in a particular geographic context. Meanwhile, it may also be interpreted as being a strategy of undermining the increasing economic and political role that China is assuming in East Asia. Yet, closer to home, India and China still have a number of unresolved border issues between them, issues which over time generate recurrent conflict scenarios among them. From an Indian perspective, China's increasing economic and political activities in South Asia do not help since India perceives South Asia as being in its strategic backyard, even though the countries in the region are not willing to accept such an Indian perception. Adding to those arguments for supporting India's hesitant position regarding the BRI is that the CPEC includes parts of Kashmir that India is claiming for itself. It is further worth pointing out that India's resistance to participating in the BRI has happened, even though BRI-related investment would address infrastructure gaps in India's northeast region which would also support India's own strategic goal of closer integration with Southeast Asia. Granted, though, it would also offer China an overland access route to South Asia and the Indian Ocean region, which again may not be so well perceived from an Indian perspective. Hence, with regard to the Indian case, its own regional and geopolitical ambitions and unresolved border disputes with China are clearly thwarting a more positive response to China's BRI.

Turning to Southeast Asia, the regional level perception of the BRI and the prospect for cooperation is a quite different, as related infrastructure investment in Southeast Asia is rather welcomed at both the subregional and the regional level. With the GMS it will contribute to the establishment of modern infrastructure connectivity within the subregion and support the subregion's interconnectivity with China. Though contributing to resilient infrastructure integration at the subregional level, this would also support integration at the regional level within Southeast Asia. Once the gap in highway and railway infrastructure is closed, modern infrastructure connectivity will link Singapore with Beijing. This in turn could generate a completely different subregional (GMS-China) and regional (ASEAN-China) integration dynamic, one with considerable economic and political consequences. But for the time being, one should not be too overly optimistic as to whether such a political-economic impact will materialise in the immediate future. This is because only the first pieces of a puzzle (individual infrastructure investment projects) are emerging, although the prospect for a considerable re-drawing of regional integration dynamics and cooperation does exist. Adding to this caution is that there have recently been some calls for the re-negotiation of already signed BRI-related investment agreements which are already in the process of being implemented. These calls for re-negotiation have been accompanied by an international chorus identifying a supposed Chinese 'depth trap diplomacy' through its BRI strategy. The two primary examples cited are those of Sri Lanka and Malaysia. Yet in both cases this request for renegotiation arose in the aftermath of domestic government changes, with the new governments taking a different perspective on those investments as, in their view, related economic and financial aspects became paramount issues. Even so, at the time of writing, those issues related to renegotiating BRI investment projects are sorted in both countries. However, those episodes should be a reminder of the political and economic risks associated with BRI investments for both the Chinese government and the host country's government.

However, the focus of BRI-related support for Southeast Asia infrastructure development also re-directs our attention to the domestic feature of the BRI, from a Chinese perspective, with its strategic aim for addressing China's continuing developmental challenges, like the imbalance of economic development among its provinces. After all, the expectation is that supporting infrastructure development with and within the GMS will also support China's Yunnan province's own development, which ranks among the rather underdeveloped provinces of China. In the past, Yunnan has for a considerable time been considered a less attractive, remote borderland province. However, since the early 1980s, there have been calls within the province for deeper integration with Southeast Asia. Yet this request for support directed to Beijing has not been well responded to for a considerable time. This changed in the context of the BRI by offering new impetus for a more prominent role that Yunnan province can take in China-GMS and China-ASEAN cooperation. The often mentioned 'bridge function' now assigned to Yunnan province within the BRI context provided ample evidence for it. Consequently this transformed the previous perception of Yunnan as being an isolated province. Certainly, Yunnan will also play an important role in China-South Asia cooperation, though because of India's reluctance in cooperating in the BRI, the prospect for further integration is, at the time of writing, rather slim. Even so, the political-economic relevance of the province for Beijing already increased, as well as promising further economic stimulus for provincial development.

A comparative case for stimulating regional cooperation and supporting the prospects for development within a Chinese province can be identified with regard to Xinjiang, another prominent case of a province strongly affected by a remote geographic location and an enduring political crisis as the border demarcations between China and the Soviet Union has not been solved until the aftermath of the Soviet Union's demise. Even more than Yunnan, Xinjiang faced an exceptionally dead-end situation, located in China's far west. Central Asia at that period in time did not offer any economic rewards for provincial development. Since then, considerable political-economic change took place. China and the newly independent countries of Central Asia not only agreed on their respective borders but as China's energy demand increased during its successful reform process, Central Asia's energy resources became a vital aspect for cooperation, not only from Beijing's perspective. Still, Xinjiang continued to face geographical remoteness from the economic-driving eastern seaboard, as considerable infrastructure gaps continued to exist. Though there also have been additional domestic attempts to overcome this situation, attempts such as the 'Go West' strategy from the early 2000s but which have only been partially successful in addressing Xinjiang's geographical remoteness. Thus, the BRI adds another strong incentive for provincial development by supporting an even closer cooperation between the new Central Asian states and China and Xinjiang and in closing infrastructure gaps between China and Central Asia and between China's eastern seaboard provinces and Xinjiang. Yet, and comparably to Yunnan, Xinjiang is also taking on a 'bridge' function but in a double sense of the term, not only with regard to China-Central Asia connectivity but also on a transcontinental scale as it connects China with Europe.

Both examples highlight the multidimensional developmental aspect of the BRI, being both domestic and international in character, and consequently the challenge of characterising it as one can identify arguments for emphasising either character. One can describe it either as a domestic developmental strategy with an international agenda attached (from a Chinese perspective) or as an international developmental strategy supporting regional integration processes in a variety of different regional settings. Yet when integrating this international developmental prospect with the potential of addressing China's own continuing developmental challenges, such as the imbalance of the prospect of development among its provinces and the developmental challenges that various Chinese border areas such as Xinjiang and Yunnan are still facing, the BRI offers a truly comprehensive developmental outlook. The Chinese government's primary goal is to support development in order to strengthen China as a country so that it can re-take its rightful place as a leading nation at the global level (as seen from a Chinese perspective). Reaching this goal requires addressing the ongoing developmental challenges that China is still facing. This is despite the extraordinary success of its reform process. Taking this into consideration, any major political-economic strategy formulated will require addressing the continuing developmental imbalance among its provinces. The BRI seems quite fitting for such a task, though from such a perspective, the BRI represents the actual version of the less successful, early 2000s 'Go West' strategy but with an extensive international focus added. A vital aspect not to be missed is that China is still at a stage in which its developmental process should not be taken for granted, even though exceptional success has already been achieved in both absolute and relative gains.

Implemented successfully, the BRI certainly will contribute to China's global rise and thus add additional input in the ongoing discussion about the implication of a rising power for the existing global order and the actual hegemon, the United States. Thus the BRI does inherit the potential of truly changing the geopolitical landscape, especially within the Eurasian landmass. This holds true, even contrary to the oft-stated claims from China's leadership that the BRI does not harbour any geopolitical ambitions, as a shift in the distribution of material power will eventually generate a political power transformation as well. After all, even when implemented only partially, the BRI will generate a dynamic shift or re-arrangement of the economic space within the Eurasian landmass and will support China's relations with its neighbouring countries. As the previously mentioned association with the historical Silk Road reminds us, there was a historical period in which the Eurasian landmass formed an interlinked economic space, even though such an interlinked economic space no longer exists. And although it would be too optimistic to predict that China's BRI will once again lead to the re-creation of such an integrated transcontinental economic space, it may offer a first and important step in such a direction. Certainly, if the BRI would be fully implemented, such a scenario of recreating a transcontinental economic space would gain more traction.

Such considerations offers a good example of how fast one can be drawn into a perception where the international focus of the BRI becomes the pre-eminent outlook, with an added focus of being interpreted as being a tool in China's strategic attempt for changing the existing international system, though this is not a perception that the author of this book shares. In addition, in countering such a perception of being a singular strategy focused on Chinese-based interests, it would also be helpful to remember that especially within the Central Asian context, Central Asian countries since their independence have been trying to overcome their geographic remoteness from the global marketplace and their infrastructure interlinkage with Russia. In this context, China's BRI, and especially the focus on supporting infrastructure interconnectivity, offers them a valuable alternative and a possible strong support for their own development. In this context, China's BRI does address an entrenched regional developmental challenge. On their own, though, the Central Asian countries are not capable of addressing that challenge. This offers a good example of the fact that the BRI does address other countries' developmental concerns. This in turn weakens the argument that the conceptual outlook of the BRI only supports China's own development goals and that only China is the country that will most profit from it. A similar argument, though on a bit weaker base, can be applied in supporting infrastructure integration between China and Southeast Asia, since most Southeast Asian countries have access to the sea. But then, closing the infrastructure gap within Southeast Asia is not only a long-established objective within the GMS process but also an enduring challenge which the ADB continues to identify. Once again, there is the implication that the BRI also addresses several national and regional developmental challenges that countries within Southeast Asia are facing.

Certainly, the discussion and controversy about the character of the BRI will continue and with it the discussion about China's rise and the implication that this will generate, although as argued throughout this book, the domestic aspect of the BRI should not be neglected. Such neglect would ignore a crucial strategic aspect of the BRI. However, we may take some caution with regard to the immediate positive economic effects it may generate for different countries, since such developmental effects will take some time to materialise. Though the positive effect for China associated with the BRI, in generating a multilateral framework within its periphery may be reached earlier and would be shaped by China's political and economic interests. Hence from an abstract perspective, the BRI may be described as a domestic developmental strategy but one with a transcontinental outlook by supporting various regional integration processes within different regional settings.

Bibliography

3rd Chairs Meeting (2018) Meeting Minutes of the 3rd Chairs Meeting EU-China Connectivity Platform. *European Commission Mobility and Transport.* Available from: https://ec.europa.eu/transport/sites/transport/files/2018-07-13-chairs-meeting.pdf [Accessed 17th April 2019].

4th Chair Meeting (2019) Meeting Minutes of the 4th Chairs Meeting of the EU China Connectivity Platform. *European Commission Mobility and Transport.* Available from: https://ec.europa.eu/transport/sites/transport/files/4th_chairs_meeting_minutes_en.pdf [Accessed 17th April 2019].

Akhtar, S. (2013) *Joint Session of ECOSOC and the Second Committee on 'Inequality, Growth and the Global Economic Outlook'.* UN Headquarter. Available from: www.un.org/development/desa/statements/asg/ms-akhtar/2013/10/inequality-growth-and-the-global-economic-outlook.html [Accessed 3th February 2019].

Athwal, A. (2008) *China: India Relations: Contemporary Dynamics.* Routledge Contemporary South Asia Series. Abingdon, Routledge.

Baniya, S., Rocha, G., Nadia, P., & Ruta, M. (2019) *Trade Effects of the New Silk Road: A Gravity Analysis.* Policy Research Working Paper 8694. Washington, DC, World Bank Group. Available from: http://documents.worldbank.org/curated/en/623141547127268639/Trade-Effects-of-the-New-Silk-Road-A-Gravity-Analysis [Accessed 15th February 2019].

Belt and Road Initiative Boosts Development in Serbia: PM (2018) *Xinhua News Agency.* Available from: www.china-ceec.org/eng/sbhz_1/t1620665.htm [Accessed 9th January 2019].

Belt and Road Portal (2019a) More Freight Trains Travel between Chongqing, Europe in 2018. *Xinhua News Agency Belt and Road Portal.* Available from: https://eng.yidaiyilu.gov.cn/qwyw/rdxw/76540.htm [Accessed 7th January 2019].

Belt and Road Portal (2019b) Number of China: Europe Freight Trains Rises in Central China. *Xinhua News Agency, Belt and Road Portal.* Available from: https://eng.yidaiyilu.gov.cn/qwyw/rdxw/76542.htm [Accessed 7th January 2019].

Bhalla, M. (2016) India-China Relations: The Return of the Sub-Region. In: Goswami, N. (ed.) *India's Approach to Asia: Geopolitics and Responsibility.* Institute for Defence Studies and Analyses. New Delhi, Pentagon Press, pp. 201–221.

Biddle, S. (2004) *Military Power: Explaining Victory and Defeat in Modern Battle.* Princeton, NJ, Princeton University Press.

Bjorn, H. E. & Derbalim, F. S. (2002) Theorising the Rise of Regionness. In: Breslin, S., Hughes, C. W., Philipps, N., & Rosamund, B. (eds.) *New Regionalism in the Global Political Economy*. London, Routledge, pp. 33–47.

Boffa, M. (May, 2018) *Trade Linkages between the Belt and Road Economies: Policy*. Research Working Paper 8423. Washington, DC, World Bank Group. Available from: http://documents.worldbank.org/curated/en/460281525178627774/Trade-linkages-between-the-belt-and-road-economies [Accessed 6th January 2019].

Breslin, S. (2016) China's Global Goals and Roles: Changing the World From Second Place? *Asian Affairs*, 47 (1), 59–70.

Breslin, S. & Hook, G. D. (2002) Microregionalism and World Order: Concepts, Approaches and Implications. In: Breslin, S. & Hook, G. D. (eds.) *Microregionalism and World Order*. Basingstoke, Palgrave MacMillan, pp. 1–22.

China, the 16+1 Format and the EU (2018) *European Parliament Briefing*. Available from: www.europarl.europa.eu/RegData/etudes/BRIE/2018/625173/EPRS_BRI(2018)625173_EN.pdf [Accessed 17th April 2019].

China National Human Development Report (2016) *Social Innovation for Inclusive Human Development, Collaboration between UNDP China and Development Research Centre of the State Council of China*, Beijing. Available from: http://hdr.undp.org/sites/default/files/reports/2783/undp-ch-_nhdr_2016_en.pdf [Accessed 25th March 2019].

China, Poland Urged to Seize Opportunity of Belt & Road Initiative for Closer Cooperation (2019) *Xinhua News Agency*. Available from: www.xinhuanet.com//english/2017-07/17/c_136448311.htm [Accessed 9th January 2019].

China's Twelfth Five-Year Plan (2011–2015) (2011) *The Full English Version, the Delegation of the European Union in China*. Available from: https://cbi.typepad.com/china_direct/2011/05/chinas-twelfth-five-new-plan-the-full-english-version.html [Accessed 4th February 2013].

Chinese Military Strategy White Paper (2015) *The State Council Information Office of the People's Republic of China*. Available from: http://english.gov.cn/archive/white_paper/2015/05/27/content_281475115610833.htm [Accessed 15th September 2016].

Chinese *Statistical Yearbook* (2016) Available from: www.stats.gov.cn/english/statisticaldata/annualdata/ [Accessed 19th May 2017].

Chongui, A. (2010) Yunnan's Bridgehead Construction Plan Brings Development Opportunities for XTBG. *Xishuangbanna Tropical Garden, Chinese Academy of Science*. Available from:http://en.xtbg.ac.cn/vtxtbg/in/201007/t20100720_56672.html [Accessed 15th March 2017].

Christensen, T. J. (2015) *The China Challenge: Shaping the Choices of a Rising Power*. New York, W. W. Norton & Company.

Clarke, M. E. (2016) Beijing's 'March Westwards': Xinjiang, Central Asia and China's Quest for Great Power Status. In: Clarke, M. E. & Smith, D. (eds.) *China's Frontier Regions: Ethnicity, Economic Integration and Foreign Relations*. London, I. B. Tauris & Co., pp. 56–86.

Communique (1978) The Third Plenary Session of the 11th Central Committee of the Communist Party of China. *Beijing Review*. Available from: www.bjreview.

com.cn/nation/txt/2009-05/26/content_197538_2.html [Accessed 5th September 2009].

Constitution of the People's Republic of China (1999) Beijing, Foreign Language Press.

Danilovich, M. (2018) The Belt and Road Initiative in the Discourses of the Central Asian States: Political Rhetoric of Growth and Academic Prognostication. *Journal of Chinese Economic and Business Studies*, 16 (3), 293–312.

Deng Xiaoping (September, 1978) Hold High the Banner of Mao Zedong Thought and Adhere to the Principle of Seeking Truth from Facts. *Selected Word of Deng Xiaoping, Volume II 1975–82*. Available from: http://english.peopledaily.com.cn/dengxp/vol2/text/b1220.html [Accessed 1st August 2009].

Deng Xiaoping (1990) Seize the Opportunity to Develop the Economy. *Selected Words of Deng Xiaoping, Volume III 1982–1992*. Available from: http://english.peopledaily.com.cn/dengxp/vol3/text/d1170.html [Accessed 1st August 2009].

Deshmukh, K. R. (2014) The Silk Road Economic Belt and 21st Century Maritime Silk Road Implications for India. *Knight Frank India Pvt*. Available from: https://content.knightfrank.com/research/1004/documents/en/silkroute-pdf-3580.pdf [Accessed 23th September 2015].

Esteban, M. (2018) Sri Lanka and Great-Power Competition in the Indo-Pacific: A Belt and Road Failure? *ARI 129, Elcano Royal Institute Príncipe de Vergara*. Available from: www.realinstitutoelcano.org/wps/portal/rielcano_en/contenido?WCM_GLOBAL_CONTEXT=/elcano/elcano_in/zonas_in/ari129-2018-esteban-sri-lanka-great-power-competition-indo-pacific-belt-and-road-failur [Accessed 14th January 2019].

European Commission (2019a) Commission Reviews Relations with China, Proposes 10 Actions. *European Commission Press Release Database*. Available from: http://europa.eu/rapid/press-release_IP-19-1605_en.htm [Accessed 17th April 2019].

European Commission (2019b) Press-Release EU-China Summit: Rebalancing the Strategic Partnership. *European Commission Press Release Database*. Available from: http://europa.eu/rapid/press-release_IP-19-2055_en.htm [Accessed 17th April 2019].

European Council (2019) Joint Statement 21st EU-China Summit. *Council of the European Union*. Available from: www.consilium.europa.eu/en/press/press-releases/2019/04/09/joint-statement-of-the-21st-eu-china-summit/ [Accessed 17th April 2019].

Ferdinand, P. (1994) Xinjiang: Relations with China and Beyond. In: Goodman, D.S.G. & Segal, G. (eds.) *China Deconstructs: Politics, Trade and Regionalism*. New York, Routledge, pp. 271–285.

Fingar, T. (2016) China's Engagement with South and Central Asia: Patterns, Trends, and Themes. In: Fingar, T. (ed.) *The New Great Game: China and South and Central Asia in the Era of Reform*. Stanford, Stanford University Press, pp. 305–320.

Gallo, E. (2014) Eurasian Union Versus Silk Road Economic Belt? *Institute for Security and Development Policy*. Policy Brief No. 159. Available from: www.files.ethz.ch/isn/184909/2014-galloeurasian-union-versus-silk-road-economic-belt.pdf [Accessed 17th January 2016].

Gilpin, R. (1981) *War and Change in World Politics*. Cambridge, Cambridge University Press.

Gordon, S. (2014) *India's Rise as an Asian Power: Nation, Neighbourhood, and Region*. Washington, DC, Georgetown University Press.

Guterres, A. (2017) At China's Belt and Road Forum, UN Chief Guterres Stresses Shared Development Goals. *UN News Centre*. Available from: www.un.org/sustainabledevelopment/blog/2017/05/at-chinas-belt-and-road-forum-un-chief-guterres-stresses-shared-development-goals/ [Accessed 28th September 2018].

Hao, Y. & Liu, W. (2012) Xinjiang: Increasing Pain in the Heart of China's Borderland. *Journal of Contemporary China*, 21 (74), 205–225.

Harmonious Society Resolution (2006) *China.ORG.CN*. Available from: www.china.org.cn/english/2006/Oct/184810.htm [Accessed 15th February 2018].

Hart, L. (1967) *Strategy*. 2nd ed. London, Faber & Faber.

Hettn, B., Sunkel, O., & Inotai, A. (2001) *Comparing Regionalism: Implications for Global Development*. Basingstoke, Palgrave MacMillan.

Hong, P. (2017) Strengthening National Policy Capacity for Jointly Building the Belt and Road towards the Sustainable Development Goals. *Department of Economic and Social Affairs, United Nations*. Available from: www.un.org/development/desa/dpad/wp-content/uploads/sites/45/publication/2017_cdas_beltandroadb.pdf [Accessed 28th September 2018].

Hua Guofeng (1979) Report on the Work of the Government. In: Main Documents of the Second Session of the Fifth National People's Congress of the People's Republic of China. Beijing, Foreign Language Press, pp. 5–100.

Huaheng, Z. (2016) Central Asia in Chinese Strategic Thinking. In: Fingar, T. (ed.) *The New Great Game: China and South and Central Asia in the Era of Reform*. Stanford, Stanford University Press, pp. 171–189.

Hui, L., Rohr, C., Hafner, M., & Knack, A. (2018) *China Belt and Road Initiative: Measuring the Impact of Improving Transportation Connectivity on Trade in the Region*. Santa Monica, RAND Corporation. Available from: www.rand.org/pubs/research_reports/RR2625.html [Accessed 29th January 2019].

Hu Jintao (2012) Full Text of Hu Jintao's Report at 18th Party Congress. *Xinhua*. Available from: http://en.people.cn/90785/8024777.html [Accessed 15th January 2013].

Ikenberry, G. J. (2008) The Rise of China and the Future of the West. *Foreign Affairs*, 87 (1), 23–37.

Ikenberry, G. J. (2014) Introduction: Power, Order, and Change in World Politics. In: Ikenberry, G. J. (ed.) *Power, Order, and Change in World Politics*. Cambridge, Cambridge University Press, pp. 1–16.

International Monetary Fund Data (2019) Available from: www.imf.org/en/Data [Accessed 10th February 2019].

Johnston, A. I. (2003) Is China a Status Quo Power? *International Security*, 27 (4), 5–56.

Joint Communique (2019) Joint Communique of the Leaders' Roundtable of the 2nd Belt and Road Forum for International Cooperation. *The Second Belt and Road Forum for International Cooperation*. Available from: www.beltandroadforum.org/english/n100/2019/0427/c36-1311.html [Accessed 2nd May 2019].

Karim, M. A. & Islam, F. (2018) Bangladesh-China-India-Myanmar (BCIM) Economic Corridor: Challenges and Prospects. *The Korean Journal of Defense Analysis*, 30 (2), 283–302.

Kennedy, P. (1991) Grand Strategy in War and Peace: Toward a Broader Definition. In: Kennedy, P. (ed.) *Grand Strategy in War and Peace*. New Haven, Yale University Press, pp. 1–10.

Kupchan, C. A. (2014) Unpacking Hegemony: The Social Foundations of Hierarchical Order. In: Ikenberry, G. J. (ed.) *Power, Order, and Change in World Politics*. Cambridge, University Press Cambridge, pp. 19–60.

Lagarde, C. (2017) Belt and Road Initiative: Proven Policies and New Economic Links. *International Monetary Fund Home Page*. Available from: www.imf.org/en/News/Articles/2017/05/14/sp051417-belt-and-road-initiative-proven-policies-and-new-economic-links [Accessed 11th January 2019].

Lagarde, C. (2018) Belt and Road Initiative: Strategies to Deliver in the Next Phase. *International Monetary Fund Home Page*. Available from: www.imf.org/en/News/Articles/2018/04/11/sp041218-belt-and-road-initiative-strategies-to-deliver-in-the-next-phase [Accessed 11th January 2019].

Libman, A. (2016) Linking the Silk Road Economic Belt and the Eurasian Economic Union: Mission Impossible? *Caucasus International*, 6 (1), 41–53.

Li Keqiang (2013) Premier Li Keqiang's Keynote Speech at 10th China-ASEAN Expo. *Ministry of Commerce People's Republic of China*. Available from: http://english.mofcom.gov.cn/article/zt_10thchina/column1/201309/20130900287593.shtml [Accessed 6th January 2019].

Li Keqiang (2015) Full Text of Premier's Speech at the 18th China-ASEAN Summit. *The State Council, the People's Republic of China*. Available from: https://english.gov.cn/premier/speeches/2015/11/24/content_281475241254129.htm [Accessed 25th March 2016].

Luttwak, E. (2009) *The Grand Strategy of the Byzantine Empire*. Cambridge, The Belknap Press of Harvard University Press.

Mahathir, M. (2019a) Mahathir Says Stalled Chinese Rail Link Can Go Ahead on 'Smaller Scale' If Beijing Agrees. *South China Morning Press*. Available from: www.scmp.com/week-asia/geopolitics/article/2180440/mahathir-says-stalled-chinese-rail-link-can-go-ahead-smaller [Accessed 4th February 2019].

Mahathir, M. (2019b) Malaysia 'Values China': Mahathir Signs Up to Xi's Second Belt and Road Summit. *South China Morning Press*. Available from: www.scribd.com/article/399754505/Malaysia-values-China-Mahathir-Signs-Up-To-Xi-s-Second-Belt-And-Road-Summit [Accessed 18th February 2019].

Mahathir, M. (2019c) Chinese by Nature Are Very Good Businesspeople: Malaysian Prime Minister Mahathir Mohamad's Exclusive Interview in Full. *South Chinese Morning Post*. Available from: www.scmp.com/week-asia/politics/article/2189225/chinese-nature-are-very-good-businesspeople-malaysian-prime [Accessed 7th March 2019].

Mankoff, J. (2013) *The United States and Central Asia after 2014*. A Report of the CSIS Russia and Eurasia Program. Washington, DC, Centre for Strategic and International Studies.

McCartney, M. (2018) The Chinese-Pakistan Economic Corridor (CPEC): Considering Contemporary Pakistan through Old-Fashioned Economic and Historical Case Studies. *The Lahore Journal of Economics*, 23 (2), 19–48.

McLauchlin, T. (2016) Great Power Accommodation and the Processes of International Politics. In: Paul, T. V. (ed.) *Accommodating Rising Powers Past, Present, and Future*. Cambridge, Cambridge University Press, pp. 293–313.

Mearsheimer, J. J. (2005) The Rise of China Will Not Be Peaceful at All. *The Australian*. Available from: http://mearsheimer.uchicago.edu/pdfs/P0014.pdf [Accessed 25th September 2018].

Meeting Asia's infrastructure needs (2017) Asian Development Bank. Mandaluyong City, Philippines: Asian Development Bank. Available from: https://www.adb.org/sites/default/files/publication/227496/special-report-infrastructure.pdf [Accessed 23the December 2017].

MOFCOM (2018) Investment and Cooperation with Countries along Belt and Road Routes in January–October of 2018. *Ministry of Commerce People's Republic China*. Available from: http://english.mofcom.gov.cn/article/statistic/foreign tradecooperation/201812/20181202815840.shtml [Accessed 7th June 2019].

Morgenthau, H. J. (1973) *Politics among Nations: The Struggle for Power and Peace*. 5th ed. New York, Alfred A. Knopf.

MRC Strategic Plan 2016–2020 (2014) *Mekong River Commission, Mekong River Commission Secretariat, Vientiane; Lao PDR*. Available from: www.mrcmekong.org/assets/Publications/strategies-workprog/MRC-Stratigic-Plan-2016-2020.pdf [Accessed 8th March 2016].

Nag, R. M. (2016) Looking East: Security through Greater Cross Border Connectivity. In: Goswami, N. (ed.) *India's Approach to Asia: Geopolitics and Responsibility*. Institute for Defence Studies and Analyses. New Delhi, Pentagon Press, pp. 143–163.

Nye, J. S. (1997) China's Re-Emergence and the Future of the Asia-Pacific. *Survival*, 39 (4), 65–79.

Ohmae, K. (1990) *The Borderless World: Power and Strategy in the Interlinked Economy*. New York, HarperCollins.

Pattanaik, K., Smruti, S., & Behuria, A. K. (2016) India's Regional Strategy: Balancing Geopolitics with Geo-Economics in South Asia. In: Goswami, N. (ed.) *India's Approach to Asia: Geopolitics and Responsibility*. Institute for Defence Studies and Analyses. New Delhi, Pentagon Press, pp. 397–417.

Paul, T. V. (2016) The Accommodation of Rising Powers in World Politics. In: Paul, T. V. (ed.) *Accommodating Rising Powers Past, Present, and Future*. Cambridge, Cambridge University Press, pp. 3–32.

Peyrouse, S. (2016) China and Central Asia. In: Fingar, T. (ed.) *The New Great Game: China and South and Central Asia in the Era of Reform*. Stanford, Stanford University Press, pp. 216–240.

Ploberger, C. (2017) One Belt, One Road: China's New Grand Strategy? *Journal of Chinese Economic and Business Studies*, 15 (3), 289–305.

Press Statements Following Russian-Chinese Talks (2015) *Official Internet Resources of the President of Russia*. Available from: http://en.kremlin.ru/events/president/transcripts/49433 [Accessed 15th March 2016].

Rajendram, D. (2014) *India's New Asia-Pacific Strategy: Modi Acts East*. Sydney, Lowy Institute for International Policy.

Rana, K. S. (2017) China's Belt and Road Initiative (BRI): Impact on Indian & Its China Diplomacy. *ICS Occasional Paper No. 16, Institute of Chinese Studies.* Available from: www.icsin.org/publications/chinas-belt-and-road-initiative-bri-implications-prospects-consequences-impact-on-indian-its-china-diplomacy [Accessed 23th March 2019].

Regional Economic Outlook (2018) *Regional Economic Outlook: Asia and Pacific: Good Times, Uncertain Times, a Time to Prepare.* World Economic and Financial Surveys, International Monetary Fund. Available from: www.imf.org/en/Publications/REO/APAC/Issues/2018/04/16/areo0509 [Accessed 10th January 2019].

Review of Configuration of the Greater Mekong Subregion Economic Corridors (2016) *November 2016, GMS Secretariat Southeast Asia Department Asian Development Bank.* Available from: www.adb.org/sites/default/files/institutional-document/214361/configuration-gms-corridors.pdf [Accessed 14th April 2018].

Sajjanhar, A. (2016) *Understanding the BCIM Economic Corridor and India's Response.* ORF Issue Brief 147. Available from: www.orfonline.org/wp-content/uploads/2016/06/ORF_IssueBrief_147.pdf [Accessed 4th March 2019].

Scholte, J. A. (1997) Global Capitalism and the State. *International Affairs,* 73 (3), 427–452.

Scott, J. & Wilkision, R. (2015) China as a System Preserving Power in the WTO. In: Lesage, D. & Van de Graaf, T. (eds.) *Rising Powers and Multilateral Institutions.* Basingstoke, Palgrave MacMillan, pp. 199–218.

Sigley, G. (2016) From Backwater to Bridgehead: Culture, Modernity and the Reimagining of Yunnan. In: Clarke, M. E. & Smith, D. (eds.) *China's Frontier Regions: Ethnicity, Economic Integration and Foreign Relations.* London, I. B. Tauris & Co., pp. 171–203.

Singh, S. (2016) Debating Physical Connectivity between India and ASEAN: Economics versus Security. In: Goswami, N. (ed.) *India's Approach to Asia: Geopolitics and Responsibility.* Institute for Defence Studies and Analyses. New Delhi, Pentagon Press, pp. 164–182.

Sonowal, S. (2017) Assam's Vision Is to Be Gateway to Southeast Asia. *India Times.* Available from: https://economictimes.indiatimes.com/news/politics-and-nation/assams-vision-is-to-be-gateway-to-southeast-asia-sarbananda-sonowal/articleshow/5910448 [Accessed 5th March 2017].

Stuenkel, O. (2016) *Post-Western World: How Emerging Powers are Remaking Global Order.* Cambridge, Polity Press.

Summers, T. (2012) (Re)positioning Yunnan: Region and Nation in Contemporary Provincial Narratives. *Journal of Contemporary China,* 21 (75), 445–459.

Support Pledged for Xinjiang (2016) *China Daily.* Available from: www.chinadaily.com.cn/china/2016twosession/2016-03/11/content_23820230.htm [Accessed 11th March 2016].

Swaine, M.D.M. & Tellis, A. J. (2000) *Interpreting China's Grand Strategy: Past, Present, Future.* Santa Monica, Rand.

Swaine, M.D.M. & Fravel, T. (2011) China's Assertive Behaviour Part Two: The Maritime Periphery. *China Leadership Monitor, No. 35.* Available from: https://taylorfravel.com/documents/research/fravel.2011.CLM.maritime.periphery.pdf [Accessed 10th January 2019].

Telo, M. (2014) Introduction: Globalization, New Regionalism and the Role of the European Union. In: Telo, M. (ed.) *European Union and New Regionalism: Competing Regionalism and Global Governance in a Post-Hegemonic Era*. 3rd ed. Farnham, Ashgate Publishing, pp. 1–12.

Tian, Q. (2004) China Develops Its West: Motivation, Strategy and Prospect. *Journal of Contemporary China*, 13 (41), 611–636.

Twenty Second Report Committee on External Affairs 2017–18 (2018) *Sixteenth Lok Sabha Ministry of External Affairs Sino-India Relations Including Doklam, Border Situation and Cooperation in International Organizations*. Lok Sabha Secretariat. Available from: http://164.100.47.193/lsscommittee/External%20 Affairs/16_External_Affairs_22.pdf [Accessed 10th February 2019].

UN Data (2019) *UN Data on Human Development*. Available from: http://data. un.org/DocumentData.aspx?q=GINI+coefficient+China&id=400#32 [Accessed 4th February 2019].

Vision and Action (2015) *Vision and Actions on Jointly Building Silk Road Economic Belt and 21st Century Maritime Silk Road*. Issued by the National Development and Reform Commission, Ministry of Foreign Affairs, and Ministry of Commerce of the People's Republic of China, with State Council authorization National Development and Reform Commission. People's Republic of China. Available from: http://en.ndrc.gov.cn/newsrelease/201503/t20150330_669367. html [Accessed 2nd July 2016].

Wang, Y. (2018) *The Belt and Road Initiative: What Will China Offer the World in Its Rise*. Beijing, New World Press.

Weerakoon, D. & Jayasuriya, S. (2019) Sri Lanka's Debt Problem Isn't Made in China. *East Asia Forum*. Available from: www.eastasiaforum.org/2019/02/28/ sri-lankas-debt-problem-isnt-made-in-china/ [Accessed 10th March 2019].

Wen Jiabao (2005) Report on the Work of the Government. *Delivered at the Third Session of the Tenth National People's Congress*. Available from: www.gov.cn/ english/official/2005-07/29/content_18351.htm [Accessed 7th February 2019].

Wen Jiabao (2012) Report on the Work of the Government. *Report on the Work of the Government delivered by Premier at the Fifth Session of the Eleventh National People's Congress*. Available from: www.gov.cn/english/official/2012-03/15/ content_2092737.htm [Accessed 7th February 2019].

Wiederer, C. (2018) *Logistics Infrastructure along the Belt and Road Initiative Economies*. World Bank MTI Practical Notes No. 5. Available from: http:// documents.worldbank.org/curated/en/259561545148936579/pdf/133058-MTI-Practice-Note-5-Final.pdf [Accessed 6th January 2019].

World Bank BRIEF (2018) *Belt and Road Initiative*. World Bank. Available from: www.worldbank.org/en/topic/regional-integration/brief/belt-and-road-initiative [Accessed 4th January 2019].

World Bank Data. Available from: https://data.worldbank.org/ [Accessed 10th December 2018].

Xi Jinping (2012) Xi Pledges Great Renewal of Chinese Nation. *English.news. cn*. Available from: http://news.xinhuanet.com/english/china/2012-11/29/c_ 132008231.htm [Accessed 6th August 2015].

Xi Jinping (2013a) President Xi Jinping Delivers Important Speech and Proposes to Build a Silk Road Economic Belt with Central Asian Countries. *Ministry of Foreign Affairs of the People's Republic of China*. Available from: www.fmprc. gov.cn/mfa_eng/topics_665678/xjpfwzysiesgjtfhshzzfh_665686/t1076334.shtml [Accessed 12 September 2017].

Xi Jinping (2013b) Speech by Chinese President Xi Jinping to Indonesian Parliament. *ASEAN-China Centre*. Available from: https://reconasia-production. s3.amazonaws.com/media/filer_public/88/fe/88fe8107-15d7-4b4c-8a59-0feb13c213e1/speech_by_chinese_president_xi_jinping_to_indonesian_parliament.pdf [Accessed 12th September 2017].

Xi Jinping (2014) The Chinese Dream. In: Xi Jinping (ed.) *The Governance of China*. Beijing, Foreign Language Press, pp. 37–70.

Xi Jinping (2018) Secure a Decisive Victory in Building a Moderately Prosperous Society in All Respects and Strive for the Great Success of Socialism with Chinese Characteristics for a New Era. In: Full Text of Xi Jinping's Report at 19th CPC National Congress, Delivered at the 19th National Congress of the Communist Party of China on October 18, 2017, Xinhua. Available from: www. chinadaily.com.cn/china/19thcpcnationalcongress/2017-11/04/content_34115212.htm [Accessed 7th February 2019].

Xi Jinping (2019) Xi's Keynote Speech at the Opening Ceremony of the Second Belt and Road Forum for International Cooperation, Working Together to Deliver a Brighter Future for Belt and Road Cooperation. *Belt and Road Portal, Xinhua News Agency*. Available from: https://eng.yidaiyilu.gov.cn/home/rolling/88233. htm [Accessed 2nd May 2019].

Xinjiang's Construction Plan (2017) Xinjiang's Construction Plan for Development of a Transport Centre on the Silk Road Economic Belt from 2016 to 2030. *Belt and Road Portal Chinese Government*. Available from: https://eng.yidaiyilu.gov. cn/zchj/dfgg/25503.htm [Accessed 27th September 2018].

Yi, Wang (March 8, 2016) China's Belt and Road Initiative Not Expansionism: FM Wang Yi. *Statement by FM Wang Yi: The State Council, the People's Republic of China*. Available from: https://nation.com.pk/08-Mar-2016/china-s-belt-and-road-initiative-not-expansionism-fm-wang-yi downloaded [Accessed 15th December 2018].

Yhome, K. (2017) India's Evolving Subregional Strategy. *Observer Research Foundation*. Available from: www.orfonline.org/research/indias-evolving-subregional-strategy/ [Accessed 28th February 2019].

Yhome, K. (2019) The BCIM Economic Corridor: Prospects and Challenges. *Observer Research Foundation*. Available from: www.orfonline.org/research/the-bcim-economic-corridor-prospects-and-challenges/ [Accessed 28th February 2019].

Zhao, Z. (1987) Advance along the Road of Socialism with Chinese Characteristics. In: Report delivered at the 13th National Congress of the Communist Party of China on October 25. *Documents of the Thirteenth National Congress of the Communist Party of China*, Beijing, Foreign Language Press, pp. 3–77.

Zhongying, P. & Sapkota, R. (2016) China-India Relations: Objectives and Future Priorities. In: Goswami, N. (ed.) *India's Approach to Asia: Geopolitics and Responsibility*. Institute for Defence Studies and Analyses. New Delhi, Pentagon Press, pp. 222–236.

Zhou Rongji (2000) Report on the Work of the Government. In Delivered at the Third Session of the Ninth National People's Congress on March 5. Government of China. Available from: www.gov.cn/english/official/2005-07/22/content_16669. htm [Accessed 7th February 2019].

Index

Printed in the United States
by Baker & Taylor Publisher Services